AFRICA PRAISE

AFRICA PRAISE

HYMNS AND PRAYERS
FOR SCHOOLS

Words Editor
DAVID G. TEMPLE

Music Editor
A. M. JONES

LUTTERWORTH PRESS
UNITED SOCIETY FOR CHRISTIAN LITERATURE

7188 1568 8

Printed in Great Britain by
Lowe & Brydone (Printers) Ltd., London

INTRODUCTION

THE idea of AFRICA PRAISE arose from requests for a book which could be used in the rapidly increasing number of schools which use English as their medium of instruction. It was felt that many of the hymns in current use are unsuitable for students in independent African nations; moreover, they lose much of their meaning because so often their thought forms are Western in origin.

As a first step a survey was made and much valuable information obtained. This established the fact that the main area of need is in upper primary and secondary schools. As one correspondent wrote: "A suitable hymn book and form of schools service are very much needed – and urgently." But it was also felt that in addition to a much more careful selection of existing hymns, use ought to be made of the rich heritage of African music. The attempt therefore was made to discover as many African hymns as possible, and to compile a book worthy to be called AFRICA PRAISE.

Part I of the book brings together a careful selection of hymns sung by schools in many parts of the world, and a collection of hymns set to original African tunes. The number of these is not as large as was desired, for the combination of African music and English words is difficult to find. Extensive use has been made of the pioneer collection of hymns published in Malawi and found in *Tunes from Nyasaland*. It has also been possible to include hymns written at recent workshops organized by the All-Africa Church Music Association at Mindolo in Zambia. The tune of No. 61 won first prize in the competition staged by East African Venture in 1967. With the Spirituals included, these hymns form nearly a quarter of the book, and so make a substantial contribution. They are to be found at the beginning of each section of the book. It is hoped in future editions to increase the number of African hymns, and further suggestions will be greatly welcomed. These should be sent to the Publishers at 4 Bouverie Street, London, E.C.4.

Part II of the book contains selected responsive readings and prayers to help those who lead daily prayers in school.

The Publishers wish to acknowledge the help given by many advisers and correspondents in the preparation of the book. Especial thanks are due to the following for comments, advice and encouragement:

> Mr. John E. Kaemmer (Director, All-Africa
> Church Music Association).
> Rev. Tom Nabeta, Miss H. Foster and Miss D. Galer
> (Uganda).
> Rev. P. Barker and Prof. J. H. Nketia (Ghana).
> Mr. Graham Hyslop (Kenya).
> Rev. R. F. Baxter (Malawi).

A NOTE ON THE MUSIC

IN making the choice of music for this book we have kept in mind the very differing cultures of African and Western music, and we have tried to exploit that musical area where the two cultures, to some extent at least, overlap.

This will not completely satisfy those who want the music sung in Africa today to be wholly African. But we must be realistic: in the vast majority of churches and schools the music is still almost totally Western, and it cannot be changed overnight. We have, however, included a good number of tunes of African origin. These tunes are liable to change as time passes, resulting in different versions of the same tune. We have chosen one such version for each hymn.

It will be noted that a few of the tunes chosen contain accidentals (17, 20, 54, 63, 117, 120); in most cases more straightforward alternatives are provided. It is for this reason that certain well-known European tunes are not found in the book.

With regard to the Helps for Worship – numbers 126–129 – the difficulty has been twofold: first, the available African tunes, being set to vernacular words, are mostly incapable of bearing the English text: second, the majority of African settings are too elaborate for ordinary congregational use. Tunes have been chosen from three different sources and in three different styles. It is hoped that they may both serve their purpose and also stand as examples of the kind of simplicity required if the congregation is to join in the singing.

A. M. JONES

ACKNOWLEDGMENTS

THE Publishers wish to express thanks to the following authors and owners of copyright who have granted permission for the use of the hymns stated below. In a few instances it has not been possible to trace ownership, and any omission notified to us will be corrected in all future editions of this book.

Miss H. M. Taylor (Nos. 1, 2, 23, 24, 45, 53, 66, 75), All-Africa Church Music Association (Nos. 3, 4, 6, 46, 123, 126, 127), World Council of Churches Youth Department (Nos. 5, 129), The Rev. A. S. Cox (No. 7), Estate of the late F. S. Pierpoint and Oxford University Press (No. 17), The Rev. R. Maxwell (Nos. 20, 60), The Rev. Dr. A. M. Jones (Nos. 22, 61, 70), Copyright Co-operative Recreation Service Inc. (No. 30), Salvation Army (Nos. 33, 34, 63, 82), Miss A. M. Pullen (No. 36), The National Society (No. 41), Oxford University Press: from "Enlarged Songs of Praise" (Nos. 50, 74, 78, 97), from "English Hymnal" (No. 67), from "Songs of Praise for Boys and Girls" (No. 91), National Christian Education Council (No. 58), Exor.

ACKNOWLEDGMENTS

of the late Mr. R. Hudson Pope and Scripture Union (No. 73), Miss H. Macnicol (No. 76), Trustees of the late Bishop Moule (No. 81), Methodist Conference (No. 88), Scripture Union (No. 94), American Lutheran Church Youth Division (No. 109), Presbyterian Book Depot, Accra, and the Rev. P. Barker (No. 115), The Rev. P. Barker (No. 117).

PRAYERS. The *Book of Common Prayer is Crown copyright* and extracts taken from it are reproduced by permission. Thanks are due to the Principal of Munali Secondary School, Zambia, who sent a copy of the National Prayer for Zambia for inclusion.

We have not been able to trace the source of some of the prayers included. Many are adaptations of existing material and have already been used in daily worship in Africa. If we have infringed any copyright we apologize and will be glad to make any necessary corrections in subsequent editions of this book.

CONTENTS

HYMNS

ix

CONTENTS

DAILY WORSHIP

GOD OUR FATHER

1

O PRAISE THE KING

Wedding Song, Malawi

In the Chorus, the tune is in the middle part

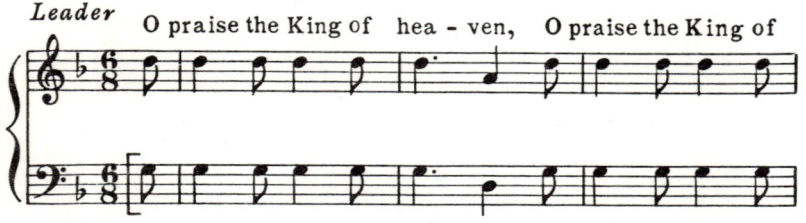

Leader: O praise the King of hea-ven, O praise the King of

hea-ven_ all ye who are his peo-ple._

Chorus

Ye prin-ces!

O praise the King of hea-ven, O praise the King of

Ye ru-lers!

hea-ven, the ho-ly gra-cious King! O

2

Ale - lu - ya!

praise the King of hea - ven

praise the King of hea-ven, the ho-ly gra-cious King!

2 L: O tell abroad His glory,
     O tell abroad His glory,
     And publish it to all men.
     Ye fathers! Ye mothers! Aleluya!

  C: *O praise the King of heaven, etc.*

3 L: O shout aloud His praises,
     O shout aloud His praises
     In mountain, plain and valley.
     Young warriors! Ye maidens! Aleluya!

  C: *O praise the King of heaven, etc.*

4 L: For He is high exalted,
     For He is high exalted
     Above all earthly nations.
     Old people! Ye children! Aleluya!

  C: *O praise the King of heaven, etc.*

5 L: For God, the great God reigneth,
     For God, the great God reigneth
     Above all tribes and peoples.
     In heaven! On earth! Aleluya!

  C: *O praise the King of heaven, etc.*

Mawelera Tembo

2

LET THE WORLD

Malawi Melody

Let the world in con - cert sing

Let the world in con - cert sing

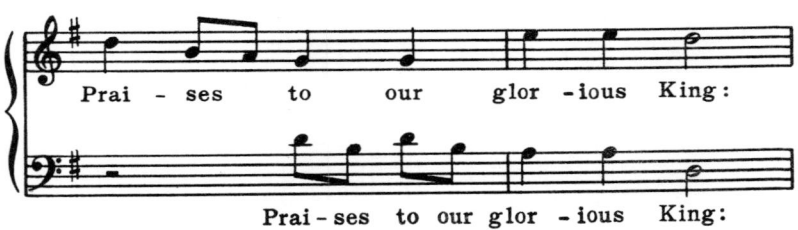

Prai - ses to our glor - ious King:

Prai - ses to our glor - ious King:

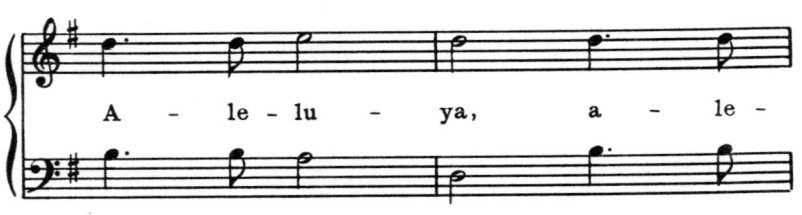

A - le - lu - ya, a - le -

lu - ya to our King!

2 Of His power and glory tell:
   All His work He doeth well:
   Aleluya, aleluya to our King!

3 Come, behold what He hath done,
   Deeds of wonder every one:
   Aleluya, aleluya to our King!

4 O ye fearful ones, draw near:
   Praise our God who holds you dear:
   Aleluya, aleluya to our King!

5 Let us now in concert sing
   Praises to our glorious King:
   Aleluya, aleluya to our King!

Mawelera Tembo

3

LET US PRAISE THE LORD   *Abraham Maraire*

Fast
Chorus
Leader

Let us praise the Lord our Ma - ker

For all the

Praise Him, praise Him,

good things He's gi - ven to us.

good things He's gi - ven to us.

Verse 1
Leader

For He gives us our food

And He gives us

Praise Him, praise Him,

good things to bless us all our lives.

good things to bless us all our lives.

*Keep on as above, except that
the Leader sings:*

And He gives us wa - ter
And He gives us sun-shine
And He gives us bree - zes   *Repeat Chorus*

Sing as in Verse 1
Verse 2
Leader

For He gives us dai-ly work   And He gives us mo - ney
                And He gives us know-ledge

So our lives are tru-ly ble-ssed.   *Repeat Chorus*

Verse 3
Leader

He gave us our par - ents   And He gives us many friends

He gives us our fami - lies   And He gives us child - ren.
                          Repeat Chorus

4

GOD OUR FATHER WE BESEECH THEE   *Abraham Maraire*

God our Fa-ther, we be-seech Thee,

Fa-ther,   we be-seech Thee, Look on us Thy children.

1 A - bide with me in my dai - ly la - bour
Con - tin - ue with me through all my life - time

Repeat Chorus after each Verse

Where peo-ple are in trou-ble please a - ssist them.

2   The Lord takes care of us when we're sleeping
    The Lord takes care of us when we're walking
    The Lord takes care of us when we're working
    The Lord takes care of us in our lessons.

3   Wherever I may go be my refuge
    Wherever they may be watch my family
    Wherever they may be watch my friends too.

4   Watch over people throughout the whole world
    Where people still are ill heal their sickness
    Where people are in trouble please assist them
    Beneath Thy wings we find strength and refuge.

5

O GOD OUR FATHER

Nigerian Melody

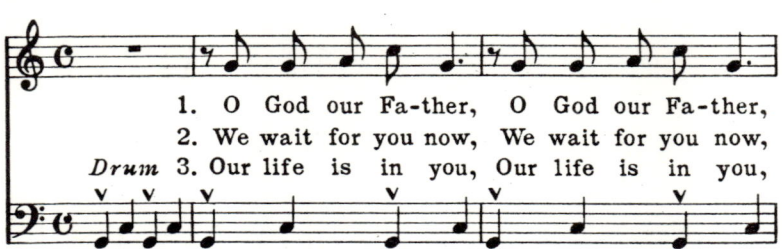

1. O God our Fa-ther, O God our Fa-ther,
2. We wait for you now, We wait for you now,

Drum 3. Our life is in you, Our life is in you,

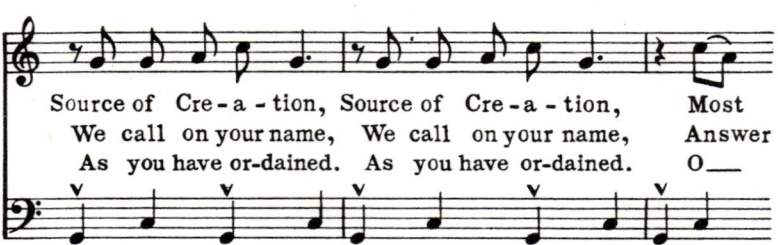

Source of Cre-a-tion, Source of Cre-a-tion,   Most
We call on your name, We call on your name,   Answer
As you have or-dained. As you have or-dained.   O___

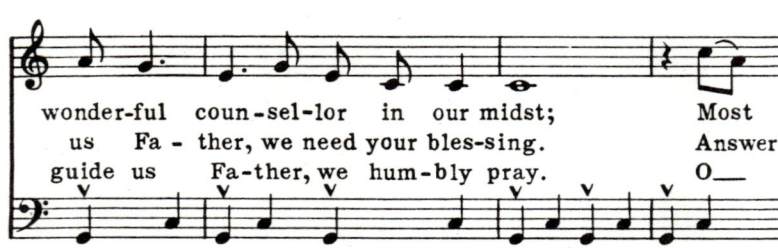

wonder-ful coun-sel-lor in our midst;   Most
us Fa-ther, we need your bles-sing.   Answer
guide us Fa-ther, we hum-bly pray.   O___

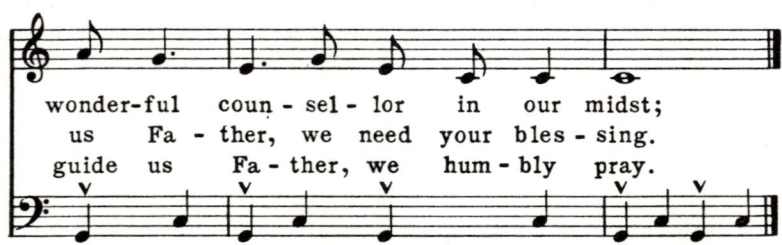

wonder-ful coun-sel-lor in our midst;
us Fa-ther, we need your bles-sing.
guide us Fa-ther, we hum-bly pray.

6

LET US PRAISE THE CREATOR   *From a hunting song*

2 It is He who gives us water
   In the fields where we labour;
   Praise the Lord of Hosts.

3 It is He who gives us wisdom
   To do the things we ought to;
   Praise the Lord of Hosts.

4 It is He who gave us Jesus
   To save us from all evil;
   Praise the Lord of Hosts.

5 If we give ourselves to Jesus
   Then we will lack for nothing;
   Praise the Lord of Hosts.

6 O, lead us, our Father
   To be with Thee forever;
   Praise the Lord of Hosts.

*Note. The basses sing "O" during the first two lines of each
verse. Trebles sing the first line of each verse and then:
"Praise to the Lord, O praise the Lord of Hosts."*

7

JOYFUL TIDINGS

Kikongo Melody

Introduction

Leader

O what joy - ful   ti - dings, great hap-pi - ness is

ours, Re - joice and be glad for the   Sa-viour has come to the

Chorus

earth from God.____ What joy - ful   ti - dings, great

hap - pi - ness is   ours, __ Re - joice and be glad for the

End

Sa-viour has come to the   earth from God.____

Verse 1

Leader

1 With won-drous love des - pite our   sin,

Chorus

Re - joice and be glad for the Sa-viour has come to the

earth from God._____ He___ sought our

Leader

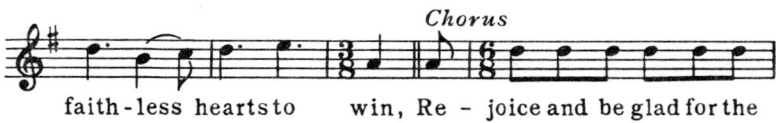

faith-less hearts to win, Re - joice and be glad for the

Chorus

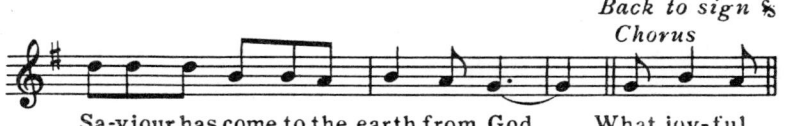

Sa-viour has come to the earth from God.__ What joy-ful

Back to sign ℅
Chorus

2 All goodly things we see or know
     Rejoice and be glad...
   From Him they come to men below.
     Rejoice and be glad ...

3 The love of God reigns all above
     Rejoice and be glad ...
   For men could not destroy His love.
     Rejoice and be glad ...

4 O Christ is King for evermore
     Rejoice and be glad ...
   Mankind in Him your God adore.
     Rejoice and be glad ...

(Repeat chorus after each verse)

Lucien Fwasi, tr. by A.S. Cox

13

8

THE WHOLE WORLD

American Negro Spiritual;
harmonised by A.M.J.

He's got the whole world in His hands, He's got the

whole world in His hands, He's got the

whole world in His hands, He's got the

whole world in His hands.

2 He's got the | wind and the | rain in His hands.

3 He's got | you and me | brother, in His hands.

4 He's got the | little tiny | baby in His hands.

5 He's got the | whole | Church in His hands.

9

The Chorale book for England, 1863

LOBE DEN HERREN 14.14.478

16

1   Praise to the Lord, the Almighty,
               the King of creation;
   O my soul, praise Him, for He is thy
               health and salvation:
     All ye who hear,
     Brothers and sisters, draw near,
   Praise Him in glad adoration.

2   Praise to the Lord, who o'er all
               things so wondrously reigneth,
   Shelters thee under His wings, yea,
               so gently sustaineth:
     Hast thou not seen?
     All that is needful hath been
   Granted in what He ordaineth.

3   Praise to the Lord, who doth prosper
               thy work, and defend thee!
   Surely His goodness and mercy here
               daily attend thee:
     Ponder anew
     What the Almighty can do,
   Who with His love doth befriend thee.

4   Praise to the Lord! O let all that is
               in me adore Him!
   All that hath life and breath come now
               with praises before Him!
     Let the amen
     Sound from His people again:
   Gladly for aye we adore Him.

Joachim Neander, tr. Catherine Winkworth

10

PRAISE MY SOUL   87. 87. 87   J. Goss, 1800-80

Unison

1 Praise, my soul, the King of hea - ven; To His feet thy

tri-bute bring;   Ran-somed, healed, re-stored, for-giv - en,

Who like thee His praise should sing? Praise Him, praise Him,

praise Him, praise Him,   Praise the   ev-er - last-ing King.

2 Praise Him for His grace and fa - vour To our
4 Frail as sum-mer's flower we flour - ish, Blows the

fa-thers in dis - tress; Praise Him still the same for
wind and it is gone; But while mor - tals rise and

ev - er, Slow to chide, and swift to bless: Praise Him,
per - ish God en-dures un-chang-ing on. Praise Him,

praise Him, praise Him, praise Him, Glo-rious in His faith-ful - ness.
praise Him, praise Him, praise Him, Praise the high e - ter-nal One.

3 Fa-ther-like He tends and spares us; Well our

fee-ble frame He knows; In His hands He gent-ly bears us,

Res-cues us from all our foes; Praise Him, praise Him,

praise Him, praise Him, Wide-ly as His mer-cy flows.

5 An-gels, help us to a-dore Him, Ye be-hold Him

face to face; Sun and moon, bow down be-fore Him,

Dwell-ers all in time and space, Praise Him, praise Him,

praise Him, praise Him, Praise with us the God of grace.

H. F. Lyte, 1793 - 1847

21

11

LASST UNS ERFREUEN L.M. with Aleluyas

Melody from
Geistliche Kirchengesang, Cologne, 1623

O___ praise Him, O___ praise Him, A - le - lu - ya, a-le-lu - ya, a-le-lu - ya!

1 All creatures of our God and King,
  Lift up your voice and with us sing
    Aleluya, aleluya!
  Thou burning sun with golden beam,
  Thou silver moon with softer gleam,

    O praise Him, O praise Him,
    Aleluya, aleluya, aleluya!

2 Thou rushing wind that art so strong,
  Ye clouds that sail in heaven along,
    O praise Him, aleluya!
  Thou rising morn, in praise rejoice,
  Ye lights of evening, find a voice,

3 Thou flowing water, pure and clear,
  Make music for thy Lord to hear,
    Aleluya, aleluya!
  Thou fire so masterful and bright,
  That givest man both warmth and light,

4 And all ye men of tender heart,
  Forgiving others, take your part,
    O sing ye, aleluya!
  Ye who long pain and sorrow bear,
  Praise God and on Him cast your care,

5 Let all things their Creator bless,
  And worship Him in humbleness,
    O praise Him, aleluya!
  Praise, praise the Father, praise the Son,
  And praise the Spirit, Three in One,

        W. H. Draper, based on St. Francis of Assisi

12

GOD OUR FATHER

Nsenga tune; Zambia

Leader ... *Chorus*

God our Fa - ther So He loved the— whole

world, So He loved the— whole world.

In succeeding verses, repeat line 2 as above.

2 L: He sent Jesus
   C: *He sent Jesus to us*

3 L: He so loves us
   C: *That He died for us all*

4 L: He is risen
   C: *He is risen indeed*

5 L: He ascended
   C: *He ascended to His home*

6 L: Risen Jesus
   C: *Risen Jesus is King*

7 L: Loving Jesus
   C: *He is caring for all*

8 L: Jesus calls us
   C: *Jesus calls us today*

9 L: Let us hear Him
   C: *Let us hear His true Word*

10 L: Let us thank Him
    C: *For He gives us His life*

Nsenga hymn; tr. by Patrick Appleford and Francis Makambwe

13

NUN DANKET 67. 67. 66. 66

Adapted from a melody by
J. Crüger, 1598-1662

Org.

1 NOW thank we all our God,
  With hearts and hands and voices,
Who wondrous things hath done,
  In whom His world rejoices;
Who, from our mothers' arms,
  Hath blessed us on our way
With countless gifts of love,
  And still is ours today.

2 O may this bounteous God
  Through all our life be near us,
With ever-joyful hearts
  And blessèd peace to cheer us;
And keep us in His grace,
  And guide us when perplexed,
And free us from all ills
  In this world and the next.

3 All praise and thanks to God
  The Father now be given,
The Son, and Him who reigns
  With them in highest heaven;
The one eternal God,
  Whom earth and heaven adore;
For thus it was, is now,
  And shall be evermore.

Martin Rinckart, tr. Catherine Winkworth

14

OLD 100th L.M.

Melody from Genevan Psalter, 1551

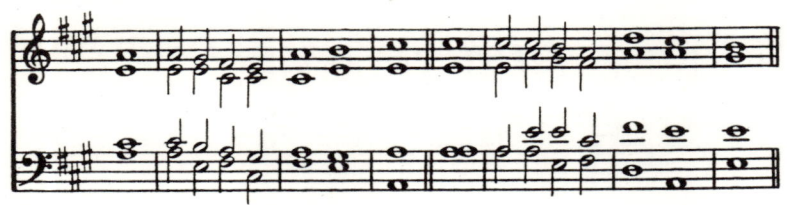

1 From all that dwell below the skies
Let the Creator's praise arise:
Let the Redeemer's name be sung
Through every land, by every tongue.

2 Eternal are Thy mercies, Lord;
Eternal truth attends Thy word:
Thy praise shall sound from shore to shore,
Till suns shall rise and set no more.

Isaac Watts

15

ANDERNACH L.M.

Andernach Gesangbuch, 1608

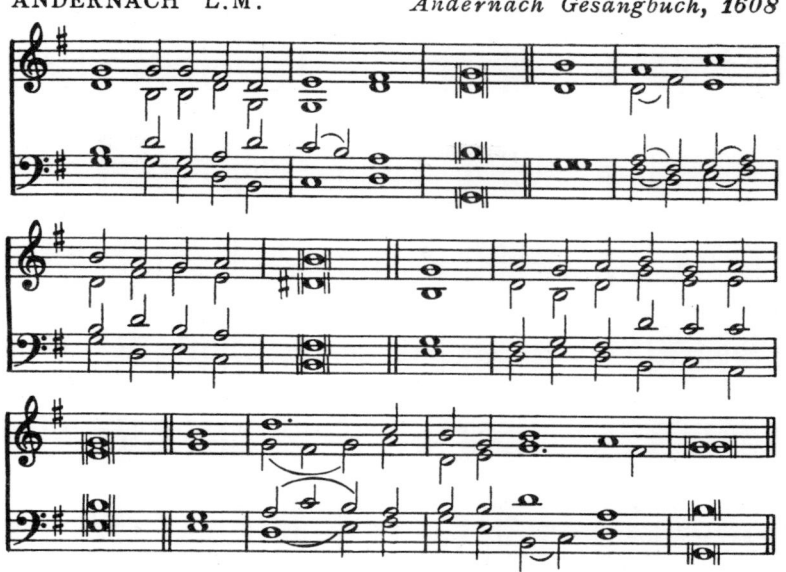

1 Yes, God is good – in earth and sky,
  From ocean depths and spreading wood,
  Ten thousand voices seem to cry:
  God made us all, and God is good.

2 The sun that keeps his trackless way,
  And downward pours his golden flood,
  Night's sparkling hosts, all seem to say
  In accents clear, that God is good.

3 The merry birds prolong the strain,
  Their song with every spring renewed;
  And balmy air, and falling rain,
  Each softly whispers: God is good.

4 I hear it in the rushing breeze;
  The hills that have for ages stood,
  The echoing sky and roaring seas,
  All swell the chorus: God is good.

5 Yes, God is good, all nature says,
  By God's own hand with speech endued;
  And man, in louder notes of praise,
  Should sing for joy that God is good.

6 For all Thy gifts we bless Thee, Lord,
  But chiefly for our heavenly food:
  Thy pardoning grace, Thy quickening word,
  These prompt our song, that God is good.

John Hampden Gurney

16

ALMSGIVING 888.4

J. B. Dykes, 1823-76

1   O Lord of heaven and earth and sea
    To Thee all praise and glory be!
    How shall we show our love to Thee,
        Who givest all?

2   For peaceful homes and healthful days,
    For all the blessings earth displays,
    We owe Thee thankfulness and praise,
        Who givest all.

3   Thou didst not spare Thine only Son,
    But gav'st Him for a world undone,
    And freely with that blessèd One
        Thou givest all.

4   Thou giv'st the Spirit's blessed dower,
    Spirit of life and love and power,
    And dost His sevenfold graces shower
        Upon us all.

5   For souls redeemed, for sins forgiven,
    For means of grace, and hopes of heaven,
    Father, all praise to Thee be given,
        Who givest all.

Christopher Wordsworth, altd.

17

DIX 77.77.77. *Adapted from a chorale by C. Kocher, 1786-1872*

1 For the beauty of the earth,
  For the beauty of the skies,
  For the love which from our birth,
  Over and around us lies,

> *Father, unto Thee we raise*
> *This our hymn of grateful praise.*

2 For the beauty of each hour
  Of the day and of the night,
  Hill and vale, and tree and flower,
  Sun and moon and stars of light:

3 For the joy of ear and eye,
  For the heart and mind's delight,
  For the mystic harmony
  Linking sense to sound and sight:

4 For the joy of human love,
  Brother, sister, parent, child,
  Friends on earth and friends above,
  For all gentle thoughts and mild:

5 For each perfect gift of Thine
  To our race so freely given,
  Graces human and divine,
  Flowers of earth and buds of heaven:

Folliott Sandford Pierpoint

18

ST. ANNE C.M.

Melody from the 'Supplement to the New Version, 1708.' Probably by Dr. Croft, 1678-1727

1   O God, our help in ages past,
     Our hope for years to come,
     Our shelter from the stormy blast,
     And our eternal home:

2   Under the shadow of Thy throne
     Thy saints have dwelt secure;
     Sufficient is Thine arm alone,
     And our defence is sure.

3   Before the hills in order stood,
     Or earth received her frame,
     From everlasting Thou art God,
     To endless years the same.

4   A thousand ages in Thy sight
     Are like an evening gone;
     Short as the watch that ends the night
     Before the rising sun.

5   The busy tribes of flesh and blood,
     With all their cares and fears,
     Are carried downward by the flood,
     And lost in following years.

6   Time, like an ever-rolling stream,
     Bears all its sons away;
     They fly forgotten, as a dream
     Dies at the opening day.

7   O God, our help in ages past,
     Our hope for years to come,
     Be Thou our guard while troubles last,
     And our eternal home.

Isaac Watts

19

ST. EDMUND 77. 77. D.   *C. Steggall, 1826-1905*

1 Let the whole creation cry,
   "Glory to the Lord on high!"
   Heaven and earth, awake and sing,
   "God is good and therefore King!"
   Praise Him, all ye hosts above,
   Ever bright and fair in love;
   Sun and moon, uplift your voice,
   Nights and stars, in God rejoice!

2 Warriors fighting for the Lord,
   Prophets burning with His word,
   Those to whom the arts belong,
   Add their voices to the song.
   Kings of knowledge and of law,
   To the glorious circle draw;
   All who work and all who wait,
   Sing,"The Lord is good and great!"

3 Men and women, young and old,
   Raise the anthem manifold,
   And let children's happy hearts
   In this worship bear their parts;
   From the north to southern pole
   Let the mighty chorus roll:
   Holy, holy, holy One,
   Glory be to God alone!

Stopford Brooke

20

ELY L.M.   *Thomas Turton, 1780-1864*

A-men.

1 Sing to the Lord a joyful song;
   Lift up your hearts, your voices raise;
   To us His gracious gifts belong,
   To Him our songs of love and praise.

2 For life and love, for rest and food,
   For daily help and nightly care,
   Sing to the Lord, for He is good,
   And praise His name, for it is fair.

3 For strength to those who on Him wait,
   His truth to prove, His will to do,
   Praise ye our God, for He is great;
   Trust in His name, for it is true.

4 For joys untold, that from above
   Cheer those who love His sweet employ,
   Sing to our God, for He is love;
   Exalt His name, for it is joy.

5 Sing to the Lord of heaven and earth,
   Whom angels serve and saints adore,
   The Father, Son, and Holy Ghost,
   To whom be praise for evermore.

J. S. B. Monsell

21

BELMONT C.M.　　　　*Gardiner's Sacred Melodies, 1812*

CRIMOND C.M.　　　　*Melody by Jessie S. Irvine, 1836-87*

1 The Lord's my Shepherd, I'll not want;
  He makes me down to lie
  In pastures green; He leadeth me
  The quiet waters by.

2 My soul He doth restore again,
  And me to walk doth make
  Within the paths of righteousness,
  E'en for His own name's sake.

3 Yea, though I walk through death's dark vale,
  Yet will I fear no ill;
  For Thou art with me, and Thy rod
  And staff me comfort still.

4 My table Thou hast furnishèd
  In presence of my foes;
  My head Thou dost with oil anoint,
  And my cup overflows.

5 Goodness and mercy all my life
  Shall surely follow me;
  And in God's house for evermore
  My dwelling - place shall be.

Francis Rous, revised for Scottish Psalter

JESUS CHRIST OUR LORD
His Birth

22

ON THE EVE

Bemba tune. Zambia

Brightly ♩.= 115

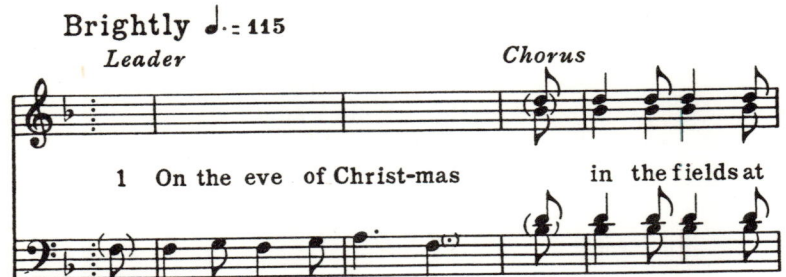

1 On the eve of Christ-mas in the fields at

night-time the shep-herds watched their flocks near

Beth-le-hem of Ju-dah: Bright an - gels ap-pear-ing

Bright an - gels ap-pear-ing, they gave the glad-some ti-dings.

2 L: "Born is now the Baby,
   C: Christ, the world's Redeemer, } Twice
         God in flesh incarnate,
         lying in a manger:

   L: To Bethlehem go ye
       to Bethlehem go ye: } Twice
       there shall you behold Him."

3 L: "Mystery exceeding!
   C: Let us go to seek Him, } Twice
         to Bethlehem returning,
         as the angels told us.

   L: The Saviour, we seek Him,
       The Saviour, we seek Him: } Twice
       mystery exceeding!"

4 L: At the inn arriving
   C: amid the lowly cattle,
         they found Him in the stable } Twice
         with Mary and with Joseph.

   L: The Saviour they worshipped,
       The Saviour they worshipped, } Twice
       kneeling there before Him.

5 L: Now on this happy morning,
   C: O come let us adore Him,
         with heart and voice rejoicing } Twice
         to worship our Redeemer.

   L: O come let us adore Him,
   C: O come let us adore Him, } Twice
         Born for us at Christmas!

A. M. Jones

23

HE WAS BORN

1 He was born a little child when He came to earth:
Angels in the heavens above told us of His birth.

Chorus: Mother Mary laid Him in a cattle stall,
Little baby Jesus, who was Lord of all.

2 Shepherds and their quiet sheep saw the angel bright:
Shepherds heard the angels singing in the night.

3 In the hills they left the lambs and the sleeping sheep:
Down to Bethlehem they came Jesus for to seek.

4 "Shepherds, whence your eager feet, running, running still ?
Who is caring for your sheep on the starlit hill?"

5 "Shall we not adore Him, lying in the hay ?
Lo, our Saviour Jesus born to us to day!"

Tunes from Nyasaland

24

GOD THE FATHER

The tune is in the middle part

God the Fa - ther,— from His throne in heaven a -

bove, Sent His Son to us in love.

2 Lo, Lord Jesus, Jesus came a Saviour then,
Came to die for sinful men.

3 Heavenly angels sang in wonder at His birth,
"Christ the Saviour comes to earth !"

4 Aleluya, aleluya to our Lord !
Ever be His name adored !

5 For He bringeth, bringeth peace to all men,
Aleluya ! Amen!

Elija Chavula

25

STUTTGART 87. 87.   *Melody by C. F. Witt, 1660-1716*

1 Come, Thou long-expected Jesus,
  Born to set Thy people free;
  From our fears and sins release us;
  Let us find our rest in Thee.

2 Israel's strength and consolation,
  Hope of all the earth Thou art;
  Dear desire of every nation,
  Joy of every longing heart.

3 Born Thy people to deliver;
  Born a child, and yet a King;
  Born to reign in us for ever;
  Now Thy gracious kingdom bring.

4 By Thine own eternal Spirit
  Rule in all our hearts alone:
  By Thine all-sufficient merit
  Raise us to Thy glorious throne.

Charles Wesley

26

SONG OF JOSEPH

Abraham Maraire

Drum

Wood block

$\left[\dfrac{6}{8}+\dfrac{2}{8}\right]$ 1 "Ma - ry please try just to hur - ry some

Ma - ry please try just to hur - ry some

1 Ma - ry, when will we be a - ble to reach Beth-le -

more. See all the peo - ple who

more. We shall not find room to

hem? Ma - ry, when will we be a - ble to

leave us be - hind, Yet I can

stay at the inn, And al - so

reach Beth - le - hem? Ma - ry, when will we

44

see   that   the   child does make you   tired
tru - ly   the   jour-ney is   too   long."

be   a - ble to reach Beth - le -hem ? Ma - ry,

2 All of the people had left them behind,
   When they arrived it was already late.
   All of the houses were filled up with guests,
   But in the stable there was room for them.
   Yet they were troubled because of Mary's child,
   To sleep there that night, and yet they had no choice.

Tenor & bass: God accompanied them while
               they were still on their way.

3 There in the stable that very same night
   The will of God was fulfilled here on earth.
   Then God did send a bright star as a sign
   To show to people that Jesus was King.
   Let there be peace among people here on earth,
   And also love in the hearts of all mankind.

Tenor & bass: Thus the will of the Father
                was fulfilled here on earth.

4 Let us now do as if in Bethlehem;
   Let us shout praises with hearts full of joy.
   A newborn baby is given to us;
   Let us thank God now for all He has done.
   Now let our hearts also be reborn with Him.
   So that we show gratitude and give Him praise.

Tenor & bass: Let us praise our Lord God
                for all the things He has done,
                Let us share with one
                another in true Christian love.

*The tenors and basses keep on repeating their words.
 In each verse (except verse 4) they sing their line six times;
 in verse 4 they sing their lines three times.*

Abraham Maraire

27

18th century melody

1   O come, all ye faithful,
Joyful and triumphant,
Come ye, O come ye to Bethlehem;
Come and behold Him
Born the King of angels:

O come, let us adore Him,
O come, let us adore Him,
O come, let us adore Him, Christ the Lord.

2   True God of true God,
Light of Light eternal,
Lo! He abhors not the Virgin's womb,
Son of the Father,
Begotten, not created:

3   Sing, choirs of angels,
Sing in exultation,
Sing, all ye citizens of heaven above,
Glory to God
In the highest:

4   Yea, Lord, we greet Thee,
Born this happy morning;
Jesus, to Thee be glory given,
Word of the Father,
Now in flesh appearing:

Anonymous, tr. by Frederick Oakeley

47

28

IRBY 87. 87. 77. *H. J. Gauntlett, 1805-76*

1 Once in royal David's city
   Stood a lowly cattle-shed,
   Where a mother laid her baby
   In a manger for His bed.
   Mary was that mother mild,
   Jesus Christ her little child.

2 He came down to earth from heaven
   Who is God and Lord of all,
   And His shelter was a stable,
   And His cradle was a stall.
   With the poor, and mean, and lowly
   Lived on earth our Saviour holy.

3 And through all His wondrous childhood
   He would honour and obey,
   Love, and watch the lowly maiden
   In whose gentle arms He lay;
   Christian children all must be
   Mild, obedient, good as He.

4 For He is our childhood's pattern:
   Day by day like us He grow;
   He was little, weak, and helpless;
   Tears and smiles like us He knew;
   And He feeleth for our sadness
   And He shareth in our gladness.

5 And our eyes at last shall see Him,
   Through His own redeeming love;
   For that child so dear and gentle
   Is our Lord in heaven above;
   And He leads His children on
   To the place where He is gone.

Cecil Frances Alexander

29

WINCHESTER OLD C.M. *First appeared in Este's Psalter, 1592*

1 While shepherds watched their flocks by night,
All seated on the ground,
The angel of the Lord came down,
And glory shone around.

2 Fear not! said he; for mighty dread
Had seized their troubled mind:
Glad tidings of great joy I bring
To you and all mankind.

3 To you, in David's town, this day
Is born, of David's line,
A Saviour, who is Christ the Lord;
And this shall be the sign:

4 The heavenly Babe you there shall find
To human view displayed,
All meanly wrapped in swaddling bands
And in a manger laid.

5 Thus spake the seraph; and forthwith
Appeared a shining throng
Of angels praising God, and thus
Addressed their joyful song:

6 All glory be to God on high,
And to the earth be peace;
Good will henceforth from heaven to men
Begin and never cease !

Nahum Tate

C

30

AMEN, AMEN

Arranged by Marion Downs

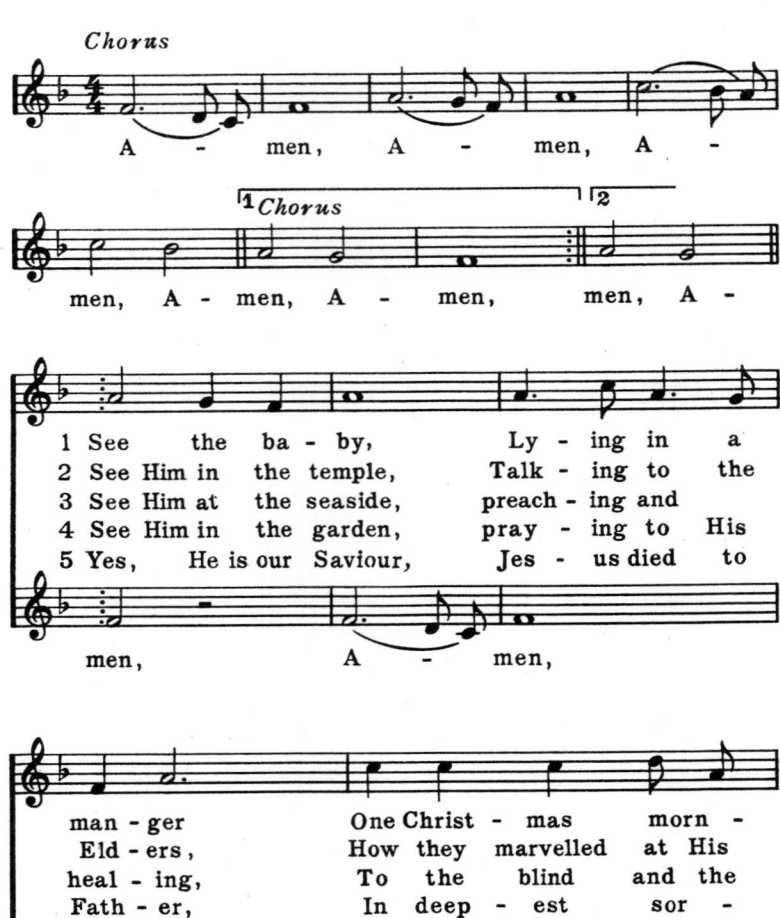

Chorus

A - men, A - men, A -

Chorus

men, A - men, A - men, men, A -

1 See the ba - by, Ly - ing in a
2 See Him in the temple, Talk - ing to the
3 See Him at the seaside, preach - ing and
4 See Him in the garden, pray - ing to His
5 Yes, He is our Saviour, Jes - us died to

men, A - men,

man - ger One Christ - mas morn -
Eld - ers, How they marvelled at His
heal - ing, To the blind and the
Fath - er, In deep - est sor -
save us, And He rose on

A - - men,

ing.
wisdom.
feeble.
row.
Easter.

A _____ men, A - men A -

A - le-lu - ya   In the king -

men.   A - men,

dom   with my Sav - iour.

A - men   A -

A - men A - men!

men   A - men, A - men!

Negro Spiritual

31

Urdu Melody
Harmonized by F. B. Westbrook

YISU NE KAHA Irregular

1   Jesus the Lord said: "I am the Bread,
    The Bread of Life for mankind am I,
    The Bread of Life for mankind am I,
    The Bread of Life for mankind am I."
    Jesus the Lord said: "I am the Bread,
    The Bread of Life for mankind am I."

2   Jesus the Lord said: "I am the Door,
    The way and the Door for the poor am I."

3   Jesus the Lord said: "I am the Light,
    The one true Light of the world am I."

4   Jesus the Lord said: "I am the Shepherd.
    The one Good Shepherd of the sheep am I."

5   Jesus the Lord said: "I am the Life,
    The Resurrection and the Life am I."

*Anonymous; tr. from
the Urdu by Dermott Monahan*

32

CHILDHOOD 88. 86   *University of Wales, 1923*

1   It fell upon a summer day,
    When Jesus walked in Galilee,
    The mothers from a village brought
    Their children to His knee.

2   He took them in His arms, and laid
    His hands on each remembered head;
    "Suffer these little ones to come
    To Me," He gently said.

3   "Forbid them not; unless ye bear
    The childlike heart your hearts within,
    Unto My kingdom ye may come
    But may not enter in."

4   Then, Father, grant this childlike heart,
    That I may come to Christ, and feel
    His hands on me in blessing laid,
    Love-giving, strong to heal.

Stopford Brooke

33

American Melody
Harmonized by F. B. Westbrook

COVENANTERS 86.86.86.

1   A workman in a village home,
     He toiled for daily bread,
     He spent His strength in honest work,
     With hands and heart and head.
     A King uncrowned, though no man knew,
     Kingly he lived, and true.

2   He healed the deaf, the dumb, the blind,
     The maimed, the sick, the sad;
     He gave to them His Father's strength,
     The radiant strength He had.
     They followed Him, a King uncrowned,
     New life with Him they found.

3   He rode into Jerusalem,
     They hailed Him, "David's Son"
     Yet, when in danger of His life,
     They left Him, every one.
     Though crowned with thorns and crucified,
     As Lord and King He died.

4   O King uncrowned, Leader of men,
     O Captain, brave and true,
     We praise Thee for Thy kingly life;
     We would be kindly too.
     To serve Thee now, Thou Saviour King,
     Our lives to Thee we bring.

Anonymous

34

MINISTRES DE L´ÉTERNEL 77.77.77. *Genevan Psalter, 1562*

1   Fishermen of Galilee,
       Mending nets beside the sea,
       Friends of Jesus, long ago
       Heard His call, and loved Him so,
       That they followed Him each day,
       Trusting Him to lead the way.

2   Sick and needy and despised
       Leaned on Him, their friend and guide,
       Seeing in that life divine
       Fairest deeds of mercy shine;
       He, their comrade great and strong,
       Turned their sadness into song.

3   Saints and heroes, far and wide,
       Loved Him more than all beside;
       Still their unseen comrade true
       Helped them all their journey through,
       And His spirit sweet and fair
       Made them strong to do and dare.

4   Many nations sang His praise;
       We to-day our voices raise
       In a glad and thankful song,
       By sweet felowship made strong.
       Jesus still our friend shall be;
       We will serve Him faithfully.

Anonymous

35

RESONET IN LAUDIBUS   *German Carol Melody*
(14th cent.)

77. 88. with Chorus

vv. 2-6 end here

vv. 1 & 7
only At His feet we hum-bly fall; Crown Him, crown Him Lord of all.

At His feet we hum-bly fall-the Lord of all. Crown Him,

crown Him, crown Him, crown, Him, crown Him Lord of all

1   Who is He in yonder stall,
    At whose feet the shepherds fall?
    'Tis the Lord, O wondrous story!
    'Tis the Lord, the King of glory!
    At His feet we humbly fall;
    Crown Him, crown Him Lord of all.

2   Who is He in deep distress,
    Fasting in the wilderness?
    'Tis the Lord, O wondrous story!
    'Tis the Lord, the King of glory!

3   Who is He to whom they bring
    All the sick and sorrowing?
    'Tis the Lord, O wondrous story!
    'Tis the Lord, the King of glory!

4   Who is He the gathering throng
    Greet with loud triumphant song?
    'Tis the Lord, O wondrous story!
    'Tis the Lord, the King of glory!

5   Who is He on yonder tree
    Dies in shame and agony?
    'Tis the Lord; O wondrous story!
    'Tis the Lord, the King of glory!

6   Who is He that from the grave
    Comes to heal and help and save?
    'Tis the Lord, O wondrous story!
    'Tis the Lord, the King of glory!

7   Who is He that from His throne
    Rules through all the world alone?
    'Tis the Lord, O wondrous story!
    'Tis the Lord, the King of glory!
    At His feet we humbly fall;
    Crown Him, crown Him Lord of all.

B.R. Hanby

36

BILSDALE D.C.M.

Gordon Slater, 1896-

Unison

1 At work beside His father's bench,
  At play when work was done,
  In quiet Galilee He Lived,
  The friend of everyone.
  Comrade of boys and girls like us,
  Playmate so straight and true,
  In all our work, in all our play,
  Make us true comrades too.

2 And as He grew to be a man
  He wandered far and wide,
  To be a friend to all in need
  Throughout the countryside.
  Comrade of men, so strong and true,
  Help us strong friends to be,
  Make us true comrades one and all,
  To others and to Thee.

Alice M. Pullen

37

St. THEODULPH 76.76. D.   *M. Teschner, 1615*

1   All glory, laud, and honour
     To Thee, Redeemer, King,
     To whom the lips of children
     Made sweet hosannas ring.
     Thou art the King of Israel,
     Thou David's royal Son,
     Who in the Lord's name comest,
     The King and blessèd one.

2   The company of angels
     Are praising Thee on high,
     And mortal men and all things
     Created make reply.
     The people of the Hebrews
     With palms before Thee went;
     Our praise and prayer and anthems
     Before Thee we present.

3   To Thee before Thy passion
     They sang their hymns of praise;
     To Thee now high exalted
     Our melody we raise.
     Thou didst accept their praises;
     Accept the prayers we bring,
     Who in all good delightest,
     Thou good and gracious King.

Theodulph of Orleans,
tr. by J. M. Neale

38

WERE YOU THERE   *American Negro Spiritual*

1   Were you there when they crucified my Lord?
    Were you there when they crucified my Lord?
    Oh! sometimes it causes me to tremble *–
    Were you there when they crucified my Lord?

2   Were you there when they nailed Him to the tree?
    Were you there when they nailed Him to the tree?
    Oh! sometimes it causes me to tremble –
    Were you there when they nailed Him to the tree?

3   Were you there when they pierced Him in the side?
    Were you there when they pierced Him in the side?
    Oh! sometimes it causes me to tremble –
    Were you there when they pierced Him in the side?

4   Were you there when they laid Him in the tomb?
    Were you there when they laid Him in the tomb?
    Oh! sometimes it causes me to tremble –
    Were you there when they laid Him in the tomb?

* *Sing* 'tremble' *three times*

39

MENDIP C.M.   *English Traditional Melody*

1   There is a green hill far away,
       Outside a city wall,
       Where the dear Lord was crucified
       Who died to save us all.

2   We may not know, we cannot tell,
       What pains He had to bear,
       But we believe it was for us
       He hung and suffered there.

3   He died that we might be forgiven
       He died to make us good,
       That we might go at last to heaven,
       Saved by His precious blood.

4   O dearly, dearly has He loved,
       And we must love Him too,
       And trust in His redeeming blood,
       And try His works to do.

Cecil Frances Alexander

40

BRESLAU L.M.

Harmonized by
F. Mendelssohn-Bartholdy, 1809-47

1 When I survey the wondrous Cross
   Where the young Prince of Glory died,
   My richest gain I count but loss,
   And pour contempt on all my pride.

2 Forbid it, Lord, that I should boast,
   Save in the death of Christ, my God;
   All the vain things that charm me most,
   I sacrifice them to His blood.

3 See, from His head, His hands, His feet,
   Sorrow and love flow mingled down;
   Did e'er such love and sorrow meet,
   Or thorns compose so rich a crown?

4 Were the whole realm of nature mine,
   That were a present far too small;
   Love so amazing, so divine,
   Demands my soul, my life, my all.

Isaac Watts

41

STUTTGART 87 . 87

*Adapted from a melody in
'Psalmodia Sacra', Gotha, 1715*

1   Very early in the morning
     On the first day of the week,
     Friends of Jesus walking sadly
     Came His resting place to seek.

2   But in Joseph's quiet garden,
     On that joyful Easter day,
     Angels told them: "He is risen,"
     And the stone was rolled away.

3   Ever since that happy morning,
     Easter makes our Sundays shine.
     Jesus, help us to remember
     As we keep this day of Thine.

G. Starr

42

Adapted from a melody in
Lyra Davidica, 1708

EASTER HYMN 77.77. with Aleluyas

1   Jesus Christ is risen to-day,
                  Aleluya!
    Our triumphant holy day,
                  Aleluya!
    Who did once upon the Cross,
                  Aleluya!
    Suffer to redeem our loss,
                  Aleluya!

2   Hymns of praise then let us sing,
    Unto Christ our heavenly King,
    Who endured the Cross and grave,
    Sinners to redeem and save:

3   But the pain that He endured,
    Our salvation has procured;
    Now above the sky He's King,
    Where the angels ever sing:

Lyra Davidica, altd.

43

WAREHAM L.M.

W. Knapp, c. 1688-1768

1   I know that my Redeemer lives!
　　　What joy the blest assurance gives!
　　　He lives, He lives, who once was dead;
　　　He lives, my everlasting Head!

2   He lives, to bless me with His love;
　　　He lives, to plead for me above;
　　　He lives, my hungry soul to feed;
　　　He lives, to help in time of need.

3   He lives, and grants me daily breath;
　　　He lives, and I shall conquer death:
　　　He lives, my mansion to prepare;
　　　He lives, to lead me safely there.

4   He lives, all glory to His name;
　　　He lives, my Saviour, still the same;
　　　What joy the blest assurance gives!
　　　I know that my Redeemer lives!

Samuel Medley

44

Anglo-Genevan Psalms, 1558

1   Crown Him with many crowns,
      The Lamb upon His throne;
      Hark! how the heavenly anthem drowns
      All music but its own:
      Awake, my soul, and sing
      Of Him who died for thee,
      And hail Him as thy matchless King
      Through all eternity.

2   Crown Him the Lord of life
      Who triumphed o'er the grave,
      And rose victorious in the strife
      For those He came to save;
      His glories now we sing
      Who died, and rose on high,
      Who died – eternal life to bring,
      And lives, that death may die.

3   Crown Him the Lord of peace,
      Whose power a sceptre sways
      From pole to pole, that wars may cease
      And all be prayer and praise:
      His reign shall know no end,
      And round His piercèd feet
      Fair flowers of paradise extend
      Their fragrance ever sweet.

4   Crown Him the Lord of love;
      Behold His hands and side,
      Those wounds, yet visible above,
      In beauty glorified:
      All hail, Redeemer, hail!
      For Thou hast died for me:
      Thy praise and glory shall not fail
      Throughout eternity.   Amen.

Matthew Bridges
Godfrey Thring

45

O PRAISE THE NAME *From a Tumbuka Wedding song*

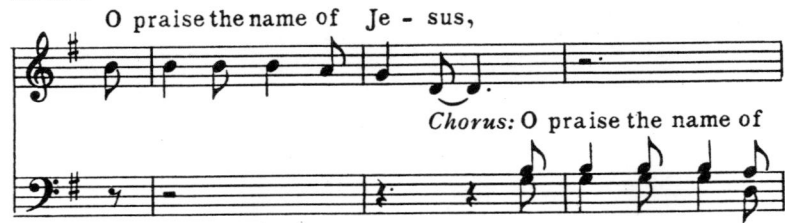

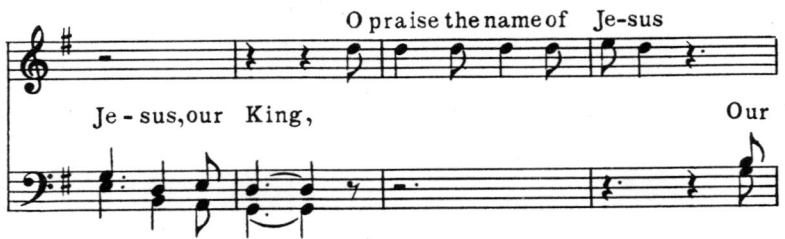

praise the name of Je - sus, our King.___

praise the name of Je - sus, our King.___

1 * O praise the name of Jesus
     * *O praise the name of Jesus, our King*
   * O praise the name of Jesus
     Our King, our King, *our King*
   * O praise the name of Jesus
     Our King, our King,
     Our King, our King, *our King,*
     * O praise the name of Jesus
     Our King, our King,
     * O praise the name of Jesus, Our King.

In succeeding verses, substitute the lines marked*
  with the following:

2 He calls you all to hear Him
     He calls you all to hear Him, our King.

3 O turn your hearts unto Him
     O turn your hearts unto Him, our King.

4 For Christ our King is coming
     For Christ our King is coming, our King.

5 Then bring your offerings to Him
     Then bring your offerings to Him, our King.

6 Come with them all to Jesus
     Come with them all to Jesus, our King.

Ben Nhlane

Note: This version of the words conforms more closely to the
music than that printed in the 'Words only' edition.

81

46

WE PRAISE HIM *Arranged by Nyakatsapa Vabyawi, Shona* [*revised A. M. J.*]

Moderate and strong

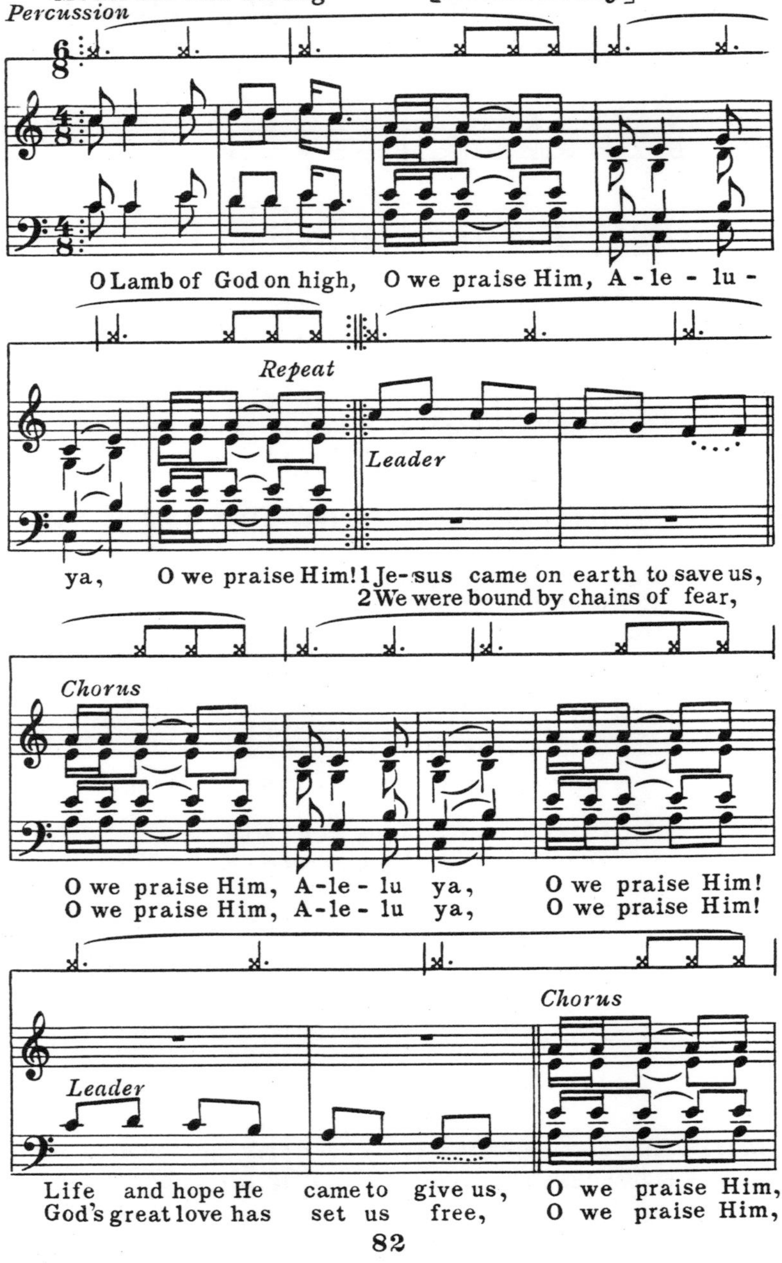
Percussion
O Lamb of God on high, O we praise Him, A - le - lu -
Repeat
Leader
ya, O we praise Him! 1 Je-sus came on earth to save us,
2 We were bound by chains of fear,
Chorus
O we praise Him, A-le - lu ya, O we praise Him!
O we praise Him, A-le - lu ya, O we praise Him!
Leader
Chorus
Life and hope He came to give us, O we praise Him,
God's great love has set us free, O we praise Him,

A - le - lu - ya,   O we praise Him!

O Lamb of God on high,   O we praise Him,

A - le - lu - ya,   O we praise Him!

3 Why did God create us men? O, we praise Him!
   Aleluya, O we praise Him!
   He created us to praise Him, O we praise Him!
   Aleluya, O we praise Him!

Shona Hymn

83

D

47

RICHMOND C.M.   *T. Haweis, 1734 - 1820*

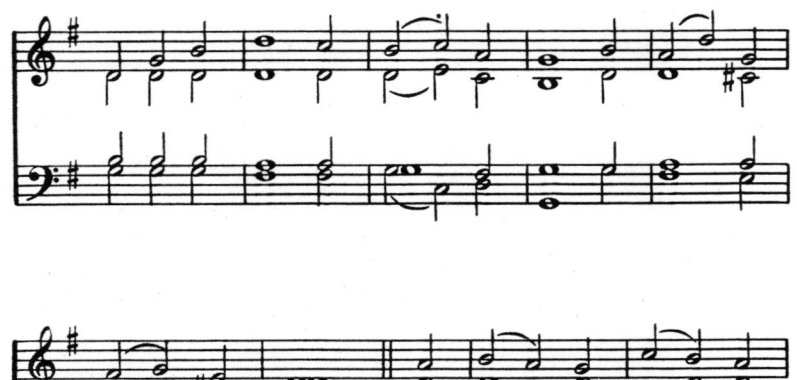

1   O for a thousand tongues to sing
      My dear Redeemer's praise,
      The glories of my God and King,
      The triumphs of His grace!

2   Jesus – the name that charms our fears
      That bids our sorrows cease;
      'Tis music in the sinner's ears,
      'Tis life, and health, and peace.

3   He speaks; – and, listening to His voice,
      New life the dead receive,
      The mournful broken hearts rejoice,
      The humble poor believe.

4   Hear Him, ye deaf; His praise, ye dumb,
      Your loosened tongues employ;
      Ye blind, behold your Saviour come;
      And leap, ye lame, for joy!

5   My gracious Master and my God,
      Assist me to proclaim
      And spread through all the earth abroad
      The honours of Thy name.

Charles Wesley

48

TE LAUDANT OMNIA 77.77.77. *J. F. Swift, 1847-1931*

CASSEL 77.77.77. *German Hymn Melody, 17th cent*

1   Children of Jerusalem
     Sang the praise of Jesus' name:
     Children, too, of modern days,
     Join to sing the Saviour's praise.

     Hark while infant voices sing
     Loud hosannas to our King

2   We are taught to love the Lord,
     We are taught to read His Word,
     We are taught the way to heaven:
     Praise for all to God be given.

3   Parents, teachers, old and young,
     All unite to swell the song;
     Higher and yet higher rise,
     Till hosannas reach the skies.

                              John Henley

49

TRURO L.M.

Psalmodia Evangelica, 1790

1   Jesus shall reign where'er the sun
     Doth his successive journeys run;
     His kingdom stretch from shore to shore,
     Till suns shall rise and set no more.

2   For Him shall endless prayer be made,
     And praises throng to crown His head;
     His name like sweet perfume shall rise
     With every morning sacrifice.

3   People and realms of every tongue
     Dwell on His love with sweetest song;
     And infant voices shall proclaim
     Their young hosannas to His name.

4   Blessings abound where'er He reigns;
     The prisoner leaps to lose his chains;
     The weary find eternal rest;
     And all the sons of want are blest.

5   Let every creature rise, and bring
     Its grateful honours to our King;
     Angels descend with songs again,
     And earth prolong the joyful strain.

Isaac Watts

50

Melody from Piae Cantiones, 1582
THEODORIC 666.66.55.3.9.   *Arranged by Gustav Holst*

May be sung unaccompanied

God is love: His the care,

Tend-ing each,   ev-'ry-where.   God is love— all is there!

Je-sus came to show Him, That man-kind might know Him:

Chorus

Sing a-loud, loud, loud! Sing a-loud, loud, loud!

God is good! God is truth! God is beau-ty! Praise Him!

2 None can see God above;
   All have here man to love;
   Thus may we Godward move,
       Finding Him in others,
       Holding all men brothers:

3 Jesus lived here for men,
   Strove and died, rose again,
   Rules our hearts, now as then;
       For He came to save us
       By the truth He gave us:

4 To our Lord praise we sing—
   Light and Life, Friend and King,
   Coming down love to bring,
       Pattern for our duty,
       Showing God in beauty:

A. F.

91

51

English Traditional Melody

1   Jesus, the very thought of Thee
       With sweetness fills my breast;
       But sweeter far Thy face to see,
       And in Thy presence rest.

2   Nor voice can sing, nor heart can frame
       Nor can the memory find
       A sweeter sound than Thy blest name,
       O Saviour of mankind!

3   O Hope of every contrite heart,
       O Joy of all the meek,
       To those who fall how kind Thou art,
       How good to those who seek!

4   But what to those who find? Ah! this
       Nor tongue nor pen can show;
       The love of Jesus, what it is
       None but His loved ones know

5   Jesus our only joy be Thou,
       As Thou our prize wilt be;
       Jesu, be Thou our glory now,
       And through eternity.

Bernard of Clairvaux,
tr. by Edward Caswall

52

ST. PETER C.M.   *A. R. Reinagle, 1799-1877*

1   How sweet the name of Jesus sounds
In a believer's ear!
It soothes his sorrows, heals his wounds,
And drives away his fear.

2   It makes the wounded spirit whole,
And calms the troubled breast;
'Tis manna to the hungry soul,
And to the weary rest.

3   Dear name! The Rock on which I build,
My shield, and hiding place,
My never-failing treasury, filled
With boundless stores of grace!

4   Jesus, my Shepherd, Brother, Friend,
My Prophet, Priest, and King,
My Lord, my Life, my Way, my End,
Accept the praise I bring.

5   Weak is the effort of my heart,
And cold my warmest thought;
But when I see Thee as Thou art,
I'll praise Thee as I ought.

6   Till then I would Thy love proclaim
With every fleeting breath;
And may the music of Thy name
Refresh my soul in death.

John Newton

THE HOLY SPIRIT OUR HELPER

53

CREATOR AND FATHER

1   Creator and Father, Thou who rulest above,
       Creator and Father, Thou who rulest above,
       Come visit us Thy people in mercy and love.

2   Thou knowest in pathways of evil we stay,
       Thou knowest in pathways of evil we stay,
       O send Thy holy Spirit to teach us to-day.

3   O Spirit, enlighten our spirits within,
       O Spirit, enlighten our spirits within,
       And show us in Thy mercy wherein we do sin.

4   To Thee do we yield us, O show us Thy way,
       To Thee do we yield us, O show us Thy way,
       To Thee do we offer our own wills to-day.

5   O teach us to do what is good in Thy sight,
       O teach us to do what is good in Thy sight,
       For all that Thou willest is perfect and right.

6   Our Father in heaven, O hear when we pray,
       Our Father in heaven, O hear when we pray,
       And grant us in Thy mercy Thy blessing to-day.

Jonathan Chirwa

54

HYMN TO THE HOLY SPIRIT

Yoruba tune
Harmony after Fela Sowande

1   Spirit of Light – Holy,
     Shine in this world of thine;
          Lighten thou our darkness, clear
          Blindness from out our minds.
     Guide Thou our ways, so may we
     Walk in the light of Thy truth,
          Come, Spirit, Come.

2   Spirit of Love – Holy,
     Fire Thou this world of Thine;
          Chasten Thou the pride of race
          Marring our common life.
     Kindle our love, that loving,
     All may true brotherhood find,
          Come, Spirit, Come.

3   Spirit of Life – Holy,
     Breathe o'er this world of Thine;
          Teach us all to know and do
          All that will make men free.
     Thy kingdom come, on earth as
     In Thy blest Heaven above,
          Come, Spirit, Come.

4   Spirit of Power, Holy,
     Mighty and infinite;
          Work within this world of Thine
          Breaking the powers of sin.
     Take Thou Thy throne, and reigning,
     Claim the whole world for Thine own,
          Great Spirit, Come.

A. M. J.

55

CAPETOWN 777. 5.   *F. Filitz, 1804-76*

1   Holy Spirit, give Thy light,
       So that I may walk aright;
       In Thy wisdom, love and might
       Guide my steps this day.

2   Keep me pure, I humbly plead,
       In each thought and word and deed;
       Lord, Thy help I hourly need;
       Keep me pure this day.

3   When temptation shall assail,
       Thou, my Helper, wilt not fail;
       Through Thy grace may I prevail;
       Make me strong this day.

4   Should my sky be overcast,
       Cheer me till the storm be past;
       Guardian be from first to last;
       Comfort me this day.

5   Make me kind to all around;
       In my life let love abound
       All Thy gracious fruits be found
       In Thy child this day.

6   Holy Spirit, who art one
       With the Father and the Son
       May the will divine be done
       Now and every day.

Mary E.J. Appleby

56

CASSEL 77. 77. 77.

German Hymn Melody 17th cent.

1   Gracious Spirit, dwell with me:
      I myself would gracious be;
      And with words that help and heal,
      Would Thy life in mine reveal;
      And with actions bold and meek
      Would for Christ my Saviour speak.

2   Truthful Spirit, dwell with me:
      I myself would truthful be;
      And with wisdom kind and clear
      Let Thy life in mine appear;
      And with actions brotherly
      Speak my Lord's sincerity.

3   Mighty Spirit, dwell with me:
      I myself would mighty be,
      Mighty so as to prevail
      Where unaided man must fail;
      Ever by a mighty hope
      Pressing on and bearing up.

4   Holy Spirit, dwell with me:
      I myself would holy be;
      Separate from sin, I would
      Choose and cherish all things good;
      And whatever I can be,
      Give to Him who gave me Thee.

T. T. Lynch

57

LÜBECK 77. 77   *Freylinghausen's Gesangbuch, 1704*

1   Holy Spirit, truth Divine,
    Dawn upon this soul of mine;
    Word of God, and inward light,
    Wake my spirit, clear my sight.

2   Holy Spirit, love Divine,
    Glow within this heart of mine,
    Kindle every high desire,
    Perish self in Thy pure fire.

3   Holy Spirit, power Divine,
    Fill and nerve this will of mine;
    By Thee may I strongly live
    Bravely bear, and nobly strive.

4   Holy Spirit, right Divine,
    King within my conscience reign;
    Be my Lord, and I shall be
    Firmly bound, for ever free.

5   Holy Spirit, peace Divine,
    Still this restless heart of mine
    Speak to calm this tossing sea,
    Stayed in Thy tranquillity.

6   Holy Spirit, joy Divine,
    Gladden Thou this heart of mine;
    In the desert ways I'll sing:
    Spring, O well, for ever spring!

Samuel Longfellow

58

EUDOXIA 65. 65.

S. Baring-Gould, 1834-1924

1 Holy Spirit, hear us;
   Help us while we sing;
   Breathe into the music
   Of the praise we bring.

2 Holy Spirit, prompt us
   When we kneel to pray;
   Nearer come, and teach us
   What we ought to say.

3 Holy Spirit, shine Thou
   On the Book we read;
   Gild its holy pages
   With the light we need.

4 Holy Spirit, give us
   Each a lowly mind;
   Make us more like Jesus,
   Gentle, pure, and kind.

5 Holy Spirit, help us
   Daily by Thy might,
   What is wrong to conquer,
   And to choose the right.

W. H. Parker

59

ST. STEPHEN C.M.

W. Jones. 1726-1800

1. Come, Holy Ghost, our hearts inspire,
   Let us Thine influence prove,
   Source of the old prophetic fire,
   Fountain of light and love.

2. Come, Holy Ghost, for moved by Thee
   Thy prophets wrote and spoke;
   Unlock the truth, Thyself the key,
   Unseal the sacred Book.

3. Expand Thy wings, celestial Dove
   Brood o'er our nature's night;
   On our disordered spirits move,
   And let there now be light.

4. God, through Himself, we then shall know,
   If Thou within us shine;
   And sound, with all Thy saints below,
   The depths of love divine.

Charles Wesley

105

THE TRINITY

60

Nsenga tune: Zambia

The bottom bass line may be omitted

(The first two lines in each verse are repeated)

1 L: Heavenly Father, Lord of all

   C: *We Thy children thank and praise Thee;*
     For Thy goodness in creation
     And the grace of our salvation
     Now are sung in every nation.

2 L: Blessed Jesus, Son of God

   C: *We Thy children thank and praise Thee;*
     Once a Cross of pain Thou bearest,
     Now a Crown of Glory wearest,
     And Thy joy with us Thou sharest.

3 L: Holy Spirit, God of love

   C: *We Thy children thank and praise Thee,*
     By Thy grace and strong protection,
     Keep us true to Thy direction,
     Fill us with Divine affection.

4 L: Father, Son and Holy Ghost

   C: *We Thy children thank and praise Thee;*
     Till in heaven with saints surrounded
     We have known Thy joy unbounded,
     And Thy praise with gladness sounded.

Original in Cilala by A. M. Jones; altd.

61

John Mgandu, Tabora

Fa - ther, Fa - ther, all of us praise Thee, We glo - ri - fy thy Ho - ly Name:

Cre - a - tor Migh - ty, Lord of all power, Cre - a - tor Migh - ty, Lord of all power we glo-ri-fy Thy Ho-ly Name. Fa-ther, Fa-ther, all of us praise Thee, We glo - ri - fy Thy Ho - ly Name.

2 Jesus, Jesus, Thou art our Saviour, *} sing twice*
    We glorify thy Holy Name:
  Give us the grace to follow thy Way,
  Give us the grace to follow thy Way *} sing twice*
    And glorify thy Holy Name.
  Jesus, Jesus, Thou art our Saviour
    We glorify thy Holy Name.

3 Holy Spirit, strengthen our longing *} sing twice*
    To glorify thy Holy Name:
  Spirit of wisdom, Spirit of power
  Spirit of wisdom, Spirit of power *} sing twice*
    We glorify thy Holy Name.
  Holy Spirit, strengthen our longing
    To glorify thy Holy Name.

4 Trinity of infinite glory *} sing twice*
    O blessed be thy Holy Name:
  One in Three Persons, Thee we adore
  One in Three Persons, Thee we adore *} sing twice*
    O blessed be thy Holy Name.
  Trinity of infinite glory
    O blessed be thy Holy Name.

A. M. Jones

62

NICÆA 11.12.12.10.   *J. B. Dykes, 1823-76*

1 Holy, holy, holy, Lord God almighty!
  Early in the morning our song shall rise to Thee;
  Holy, holy, holy, merciful and mighty,
  God in three Persons, blessèd Trinity!

2 Holy, holy, holy! all the saints adore Thee,
  Casting down their golden crowns around the glassy sea;
  Cherubim and seraphim falling down before Thee,
  Who wast, and art, and evermore shalt be.

3 Holy, holy, holy! though the darkness hide Thee,
  Though the eye of sinful man Thy glory may not see,
  Only Thou art holy; there is none beside Thee
  Perfect in power, in love, and purity.

4 Holy, holy, holy, Lord God almighty!
  All Thy works shall praise Thy name, in earth, and sky,
                                              and sea:
  Holy, holy, holy, merciful and mighty,
  God in three Persons, blessèd Trinity!

Reginald Heber

63

ERFREUT EUCH 7676. D

German Melody, 1536

1   We praise Thee, Heavenly Father
        For all Thy tender care;
Rich tokens of Thy mercy
        And love are everywhere,
Thou art from everlasting,
        And ever shalt endure;
Throughout unending ages
        Thy promises are sure.

2   We praise Thy name, Lord Jesus,
        Thou art the Christ divine;
No sacrificial offering
        Can e'er compare with Thine,
Living Thy life for others,
        Then dying on the tree
To rise again triumphant
        In glorious majesty.

3   We praise Thee, Holy Spirit,
        Revealer of the truth;
Seal us Thine own, we pray Thee,
        In these glad days of youth.
Equip for joyful service,
        Arm us with holy might,
Give victory in temptation
        And courage for the fight.

4   We worship and adore Thee,
        Blest Trinity above;
Our lives we gladly yield Thee
        As tokens of our love.
Thine own we now restore Thee,
        Our wills to Thee resign;
Accept our grateful offerings
        And make us fully Thine.

Walter H. Windybank

THE CHURCH

64

ITS NATURE AND PURPOSE

TRES MAGI DE GENTIBUS 777. 6

Andernach Gesangbuch, 1608

1   Jesus, with Thy Church abide;
    Be her Saviour, Lord, and guide,
    While on earth her faith is tried:
      We beseech Thee, hear us.

2   Keep her life and doctrine pure;
    Grant her patience to endure,
    Trusting in Thy promise sure:
      We beseech Thee, hear us.

3   May her voice be ever clear,
    Warning of a judgment near,
    Telling of a Saviour dear:
      We beseech Thee, hear us.

4   May she one in doctrine be,
    One in truth and charity,
    Winning all to faith in Thee:
      We beseech Thee, hear us.

5   May she guide the poor and blind,
    Seek the lost until she find,
    And the broken-hearted bind:
      We beseech Thee, hear us.

6   May she holy triumphs win,
    Overthrow the hosts of sin,
    Gather all the nations in:
      We beseech Thee, hear us.

T. B. Pollock

65

ES FLOG EIN KLEINS WALDVÖGELEIN 76.76.D

German Tradtional Melody

AURELIA 76.76.D

S.S. Wesley, 1810-76

1   The Church's one foundation
Is Jesus Christ her Lord:
She is His new creation
By water and the word:
From heaven He came and sought her
To be His holy bride;
With His own blood He bought her,
And for her life He died.

2   Elect from every nation,
Yet one o'er all the earth,
Her charter of salvation
One Lord, one faith, one birth,
One holy name she blesses,
Partakes one holy food,
And to one hope she presses,
With every grace endued.

3   Mid toil and tribulation,
And tumult of her war,
She waits the consummation
Of peace for evermore;
Till with the vision glorious
Her longing eyes are blest,
And the great Church victorious
Shall be the Church at rest.

4   Yet she on earth hath union
With God the Three in One,
And mystic sweet communion
With those whose rest is won.
O happy ones and holy!
Lord, give us grace that we,
Like them, the meek and lowly,
On high may dwell with Thee.

S. J. Stone

WE REMEMBER THEE

1   We remember Thee, Lord Jesus,
Thou didst die for us on the tree:
Hear us now when we cry to Thee.

2   We remember Thee, Lord Jesus,
For Thy life's blood was shed in pain,
And Thy body for us was slain

3   We remember Thee, Lord Jesus,
When we taste of the bread and wine;
In this sacrament make us Thine.

Thomas Ngoma

67

ACH GOTT UND HERR 87. 87, Iambic

Harmonised by
J. S. Bach, 1685-1750

1   Strengthen for service, Lord, the hands
      That holy things have taken;
    Let ears that now have heard Thy songs
      To clamour never waken.

2   Lord, may the tongues which "Holy" sang
      Keep free from all deceiving;
    The eyes which saw Thy love be bright,
      Thy blessed hope perceiving.

3   The feet that tread Thy holy courts
      From light do Thou not banish;
    The bodies by Thy body fed
      With Thy new life replenish.

Liturgy of Malabar,
tr. C. W. Humphreys, Percy Dearmer

68

BELMONT C.M.   *Gardiner's Sacred Melodies, 1812*

1   Be known to us in breaking bread,
         But do not then depart;
     Saviour, abide with us, and spread
         Thy table in our heart.

2   There sup with us in love divine;
         Thy body and Thy blood,
     That living bread, that heavenly wine,
         Be our immortal food.

James Montgomery

69

MARIA JUNG UND ZART 66.66.

'Psalteriolum Harmonicum', 1642

1   I hunger and I thirst;
    Jesus, my manna be;
    Ye living waters, burst
      Out of the rock for me.

2   Thou bruised and broken Bread,
      My life-long wants supply;
    As living souls are fed,
      O feed me, or I die.

3   Thou true life-giving Vine,
      Let me Thy sweetness prove;
    Renew my life with Thine,
      Refresh my soul with love.

4   Rough paths my feet have trod,
      Since first their course began;
    Feed me, Thou Bread of God;
      Help me, Thou Son of Man.

5   For still the desert lies
      My fainting soul before;
    O living waters rise
      Within me evermore.

J. S. B. Monsell

121

THE CHRISTIAN LIFE

70

Reading the Bible

WORD OF GOD

Yoruba tune, West Africa
after Fela Sowande

♩. = 90

1   Blessed Word of God
    Blessed Word of God,
       Light of the faltering steps of men,
    Blessed Word of God.

2   Holy Word of God
    Holy Word of God,
       Drawing our hearts up to God above,
    Holy Word of God.

3   Sweetest Word of God
    Sweetest Word of God,
       Message of Love coming down from Heav'n,
    Sweetest Word of God.

4   Word of sins forgiven
    Word of sins forgiven,
       Word of salvation's redeeming love,
    Word of sins forgiven.

5   Word of Truth and Life
    Word of Truth and Life,
       Teaching of Jesus, our Way and Guide,
    Word of Truth and Life.

6   Joyous Word of God
    Joyous Word of God,
       Leading us all to the joys of Heav'n,
    Joyous Word of God.

A. M. Jones

71

ST. MARTIN 66.66.   *C. Ett, Cantica Sacra, 1840*

1   Lord, Thy word abideth,
And our footsteps guideth,
Who its truth believeth
Light and joy receiveth.

2   When our foes are near us,
Then Thy word doth cheer us,
Word of consolation.
Message of salvation.

3   When the storms are o'er us,
And dark clouds before us,
Then its light directeth,
And our way protecteth.

4   Who can tell the pleasure,
Who recount the treasure,
By Thy word imparted
To the simple-hearted?

5   Word of mercy, giving
Succour to the living;
Word of life, supplying
Comfort to the dying!

6   O that we, discerning
Its most holy learning,
Lord, may love and fear Thee,
Evermore be near Thee!

Henry Williams Baker

72

FFIGYSBREN 10.10.10.10.   *Welsh Hymn Melody, 1840*

1 Break Thou the bread of life, dear Lord, to me,
As Thou didst break the loaves beside the sea:
Beyond the sacred page I seek Thee, Lord;
My spirit pants for Thee, O living Word!

2 Thou art the Bread of Life, dear Lord, to me,
Thy holy word the truth that saveth me:
Give me to eat and live with Thee above;
Teach me to love Thy truth, for Thou art love.

3 O send Thy Spirit, Lord, now unto me,
That He may touch my eyes, and make me see:
Show me the truth concealed within Thy word,
And in Thy Book revealed I see Thee, Lord.

Mary Artemisia Lathbury (*v. 1*);
Alexander Groves (*vv. 2, 3*)

73

ST. MICHAEL S.M.   *Genevan Psalter, 1551*

1   We thank Thee, Lord, indeed,
     That Thou Thy Word hast given,
     To light our path in this dark world,
     And safely guide to Heaven.

2   To warn of sinful **steps**,
     And point our road each day,
     To keep us in the one safe path,
     The strait and narrow way.

3   Bless those who with us read
     Thy wondrous Book of Light,
     That all of us with one desire
     May strive to do the right.

4   As Thy commands we seek
     Within Thy Word each day,
     Teach us what Thou wilt have us do,
     Then teach us to obey.

5   Oh, give us minds to learn,
     And hearts to know Thy will,
     And make us willing, cheerful, strong,
     Thy bidding to fulfil!

6   We feel our weakness, Lord,
     But knowing Thou art near,
     When we are weak, then we are strong,
     We need not, will not, fear.

R. Hudson Pope

74

J. R. Ahle, 1625-73

1   Book of books, our people's strength,
    Statesman's, teacher's, hero's treasure,
    Bringing freedom, spreading truth,
    Shedding light that none can measure —
    Wisdom comes to those who know Thee,
    All the best we have we owe Thee.

2   Thank we those who toiled in thought,
    Many diverse scrolls completing,
    Poets, prophets, scholars, saints,
    Each his word from God repeating;
    Till they came, who told the story
    Of the Word, and showed His glory.

3   Praise we God, who hath inspired
    Those whose wisdom still directs us,
    Praise Him for the Word made flesh,
    For the Spirit who protects us.
    Light of knowledge, ever burning,
    Shed on us Thy deathless learning.

P. Dearmer

131

75

WHEN I CALLED   *Wedding Song, Malawi*

When three parts sing, the main tune is in the middle part

When I called to Je-sus When I called to

Je-sus He an-swered me in love.

love. He is my Sa - viour, He is my

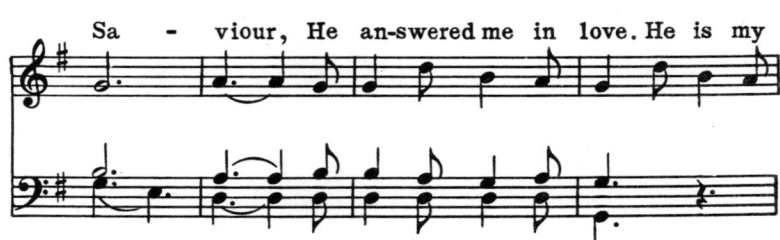

Sa - viour, He an-swered me in love. He is my

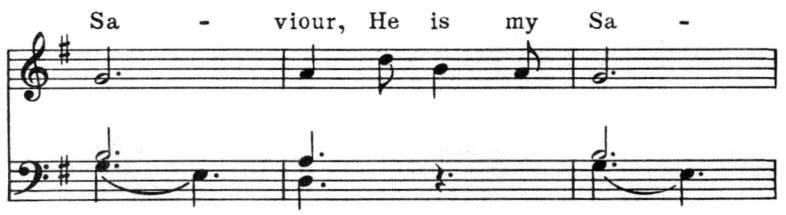

Sa - viour, He is my Sa -

viour, — He an-swered me in love.

2 L: When I prayed for mercy
   C: When I prayed for mercy He answered
      me in love.

   (whole verse to be repeated)
   Chorus

3 L: When I cried unto Him
   C: When I cried unto Him He answered
      me in love.

   (whole verse to be repeated)
   Chorus

4 L: When I came to Jesus
   C: When I came to Jesus He answered
      me in love.

   (whole verse to be repeated)
   Chorus

Mawelera Tembo

76

FINGAL C.M.

Adapted J. S. Anderson & A. M. J.

1   One who is quite unfit to be
        A scholar in Thy school,
     Thou in Thy love hast called me "friend"-
        O kindness wonderful !

2   So weak am I, O gracious Lord,
        So poor in will and deed :
     My only hope is for Thy grace
        To help me in my need.

3   When in His flesh they drove the nails,
        Did He not all endure ?
     What one of us is worthy of
        A life so great and pure ?

4   He, Love itself in human form,
        For love of me He came :
     My answer to His love must be
        To glorify His Name.

5   If anything is good in me
        It comes from Thee above:
     Then strengthen me to serve Thee, Lord,
        That serving, I may love.

Adapted from Narayan Vaman Tilak,
tr. Nicol Macnicol

77

STEAL AWAY

American Negro Spiritual

Steal a-way, steal a-way, steal a-way to Je - sus, steal a-way, steal a-way home, I ain't got long to stay here. My Lord calls me, He calls me by the thun-der, The trum-pet sounds with-

136

in-a my soul, I ain't got long to stay here.

2 Green trees are bending, poor sinner stands a-trembling;
The trumpet sounds within-a my soul!
I ain't got long to stay here.

3 My Lord calls me, He calls me by the lightning;
The trumpet sounds within-a my soul!
I ain't got long to stay here.

78

NOTTINGHAM 77.77

School of Mozart

1 In our work and in our play,
  Jesus, ever with us stay;
  May we always strive to be
  True and faithful unto Thee.

2 May we in Thy strength subdue
  Evil tempers, words untrue,
  Thoughts impure and deeds unkind,
  All things hateful to Thy mind.

3 Jesus, from Thy throne above
  Deign to fill us with Thy love,
  So that all around may see
  We belong, dear Lord, to Thee.

4 Children of the King are we,
  May we loyal to Him be,
  Try to please Him every day
  In our work and in our play.

Whitfield Glanville Wills

138

79

NORTH COATES 65.65   *T. R. Matthews, 1826-1910*

1 Jesus, high in glory,
  Lend a listening ear;
 When we bow before Thee,
  Children's praises hear

2 Though Thou art so holy,
  Heaven's almighty King,
 Thou wilt stoop to listen
  When Thy praise we sing.

3 Save us, Lord, from sinning,
  Watch us day by day;
 Help us now to love Thee;
  Take our sins away.

4 Strengthen us for duty
  While on earth we live;
 May we to Thy service
  Our best talents give.

Harriet M'Keever

80

WYCHBOLD 87. 87   *W. G. Whinfield, 1865-1919*

1   Day by day we magnify Thee,
      When, as each new day is born,
    On our knees at home, we bless Thee
      For the mercies of the morn.

2   Day by day we magnify Thee,
      When our hymns in school we raise,
    Daily work begun and ended
      With the daily voice of praise.

3   Day by day we magnify Thee,
      Not in words of praise alone;
    Truthful lips and meek obedience
      Show Thy glory in Thine own.

4   Day by day we magnify Thee,
      When for Jesus' sake we try
    Every wrong to bear with patience,
      Every sin to mortify.

5   Day by day we magnify Thee,
      Till our days on earth shall cease,
    Till we rest from these our labours,
      Waiting for Thy day in peace.

John Ellerton

81

BOYCE 77. 77

W. Boyce 1710 - 79

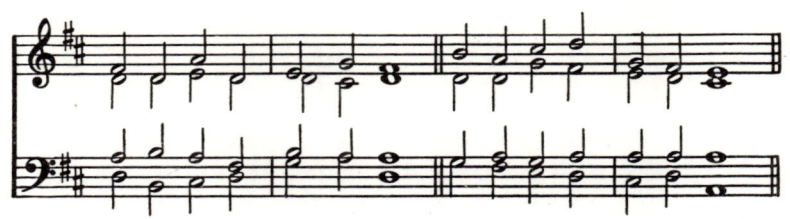

1   Lord and Saviour, true and kind,
    Be the master of my mind;
    Bless and guide and strengthen still
    All my powers of thought and will.

2   While I ply the scholar's task
    Jesus Christ, be near, I ask;
    Help the memory, clear the brain,
    Knowledge still to seek and gain.

3   Here I train for life's swift race;
    Let me do it in Thy grace:
    Here I arm me for life's fight;
    Let me do it in Thy might.

4   Thou hast made me mind and soul;
    I for Thee would use the whole:
    Thou hast died that I might live,
    All my powers to Thee I give.

5   Striving, thinking, learning still ,
    Let me follow thus Thy will,
    Till my whole glad nature be
    Trained for duty and for Thee.

Handley Carr Glyn Moule

82

TALLIS' ORDINAL C.M.　　　　　*Thomas Tallis c. 1505-85*

1　O Saviour, who wast once a child,
　　We pray that we may be
　　In every thought and word and deed
　　Inspired and led by Thee.

2　O help us to apply our minds
　　To study day by day;
　　Didst Thou not in the Temple court
　　For strength and wisdom pray?

3　O help us to be witnesses
　　To school friends that we meet;
　　So they may see in us the power
　　That never knows defeat.

4　O help us keep our hearts and minds
　　From all uncleanness free,
　　That temples of the living God
　　We truly, Lord, may be

Peter M. Cooke

83

HARTS 77.77

B. Milgrove, 1731-1810

1 Saviour, teach me, day by day,
  Love's sweet lesson to obey;
  Sweeter lesson cannot be,
  Loving Him Who first loved me.

2 Teach me, I am not my own,
  I am Thine, and Thine alone;
  Thine to keep, to rule, to save
  From all sin that would enslave.

3 With a child's glad heart of love
  At Thy bidding may I move.
  Prompt to serve and follow Thee,
  Loving Him Who first loved me.

4 Teach me thus Thy steps to trace,
  Strong to follow in Thy grace,
  Learning how to love from Thee,
  Loving Him Who first loved me.

Jane Leeson

84

ST. JAMES C.M.

R. Courteville, ? 1677-1772

1   Thou art the Way: to Thee alone
     From sin and death we flee:
     And he who would the Father seek
     Must seek Him, Lord, by Thee.

2   Thou art the Truth: Thy word alone
     True wisdom can impart;
     Thou only can inform the mind
     And purify the heart.

3   Thou art the Life: the rending tomb
     Proclaims Thy conquering arm;
     And those who put their trust in Thee
     Nor death nor hell shall harm.

4   Thou art the Way, the Truth, the Life:
     Grant us that Way to know,
     That Truth to keep, that Life to win,
     Whose joys eternal flow.

George Washington Doane

F

85

ST MARTIN 77. 77   *Old French Melody*

1 Father, lead me day by day,
   Ever in Thine own good way;
   Teach me to be pure and true,
   Show me what I ought to do.

2 When in danger, make me brave;
   Make me know that Thou canst save.
   Keep me safe by Thy dear side;
   Let me in Thy love abide.

3 When I'm tempted to do wrong,
   Make me steadfast, wise, and strong;
   And when all alone I stand,
   Shield me with Thy mighty hand.

4 When my heart is full of glee,
   Help me to remember Thee;
   Happy most of all to know
   That my Father loves me so.

5 When my work seems hard and dry,
   May I press on cheerily;
   Help me patiently to bear
   Pain and hardship, toil and care.

6 May I do the good I know,
   Be Thy loving child below,
   Then at last go home to Thee
   Evermore Thy child to be.

J. P. Hopps

86

ORIEL 87. 87. 87.   *C. Ett, Cantica Sacra, 1840*

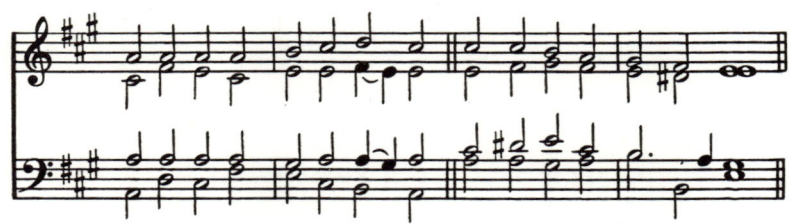

1 Lead us, heavenly Father, lead us
    O'er the world's tempestuous sea;
  Guard us, guide us, keep us, feed us,
    For we have no help but Thee;
  Yet possessing every blessing
    If our God our Father be.

2 Saviour, breathe forgiveness o'er us;
    All our weakness Thou dost know,
  Thou didst tread this earth before us,
    Thou didst feel its keenest woe;
  Lone and dreary, faint and weary,
    Through the desert Thou didst go.

3 Spirit of our God, descending,
    Fill our hearts with heavenly joy,
  Love with every passion blending,
    Pleasure that can never cloy:
  Thus provided, pardoned, guided,
    Nothing can our peace destroy.

James Edmeston

87

TRUST AND OBEY 669.D with Refrain

D.B. Towner, 1850 - 1919

Refrain

1   When we walk with the Lord
    In the light of His Word
    What a glory He sheds on our way!
    While we do His good will
    He abides with us still,
    And with all who will trust and obey.

        Trust and obey, for there's no other way
        To be happy in Jesus,
        But to trust and obey.

2   Not a shadow can rise,
    Not a cloud in the skies,
    But His smile quickly drives it away;
    Not a doubt nor a fear,
    Not a sigh nor a tear,
    Can abide while we trust and obey.

3   Not a burden we bear,
    Not a sorrow we share,
    But our toil He doth richly repay;
    Not a grief nor a loss,
    Not a frown nor a cross,
    But is blest if we trust and obey.

4   But we never can prove
    The delights of His love
    Until all on the altar we lay;
    For the favour He shows,
    And the joy He bestows,
    Are for them who will trust and obey.

5   Then in fellowship sweet
    We will sit at His feet,
    Or we'll walk by His side in the way;
    What He says we will do,
    Where He sends we will go –
    Never fear, only trust and obey.

                    John Henry Sammis

                        153

88

CAMBER 65.65.

Martin Shaw, 1875-1958

1   Wise men seeking Jesus
    Travelled from afar,
    Guided on their journey
    By a beauteous star.

2   But if we desire Him,
    He is close at hand;
    For our native country
    Is our Holy Land.

3   Prayerful souls may find Him
    By our quiet lakes,
    Meet Him on our hillsides
    When the morning breaks.

4   Fishermen talk with Him
    By the mighty sea,
    As the first disciples
    Did in Galilee.

5   Every peaceful village
    In our land might be
    Made by Jesus' presence
    Like sweet Bethany.

6   He is more than near us,
    If we love Him well;
    For He seeketh ever
    In our hearts to dwell.

J. T. East

89

PEARSALL 76. 76. D

R. L. de Pearsall, 1795 - 1856

1   The wise may bring their learning,
     The rich may bring their wealth;
And some may bring their greatness,
     And some bring strength and health;
We too would bring our treasures
     To offer to the King:
We have no wealth or learning –
     What shall we children bring?

2   We'll bring Him hearts that love Him,
     We'll bring Him thankful praise,
And young souls meekly striving
     To walk in holy ways:
And these shall be the treasures
     We offer to the King,
And these are gifts that even
     The poorest child may bring

3   We'll bring the little duties
     We have to do each day,
We'll try our best to please Him
     At home, at school, at play:
And better are these treasures
     To offer to our King
Than richest gifts without them;
     Yet these a child may bring.

Book of Praise for Children, altd.

90

FRANCONIA S.M.   *Arr. by W. H. Havergal, 1793 - 1870*

1 Blest are the pure in heart,
   For they shall see their God;
   The secret of the Lord is theirs;
   Their soul is Christ's abode.

2 The Lord who left the heavens
   Our life and peace to bring,
   To dwell in lowliness with men,
   Their pattern and their king:

3 Still to the lowly soul
   He doth Himself impart,
   And for His dwelling and His throne
   Chooseth the pure in heart.

4 Lord, we Thy presence seek:
   May ours this blessing be;
   Give us a pure and lowly heart,
   A temple meet for Thee.

John Keble,
William John Hall

91

Melody from J. H. Knecht, 1752 - 1817

1   God my Father, loving me,
         Gave His Son my friend to be:
         Gave His Son, my form to take,
         And to suffer for my sake.

2   Jesus still remains the same
         As in days of old He came;
         As my brother by my side,
         Still He seeks my steps to guide.

3   How can I repay Thy love,
         Lord of all the hosts above ?
         What have I, a child, to bring
         Unto Thee, Thou heavenly King ?

4   I have but myself to give,
         Let me to Thy glory live;
         Let me follow, day by day,
         Where Thou showest me the way.

G. W. Briggs

92

VERULAMIUM   *A. M. Jones*

1   May the mind of Christ my Saviour
Live in me from day to day,
By His love and power controlling
All I do or say.

2   May the Word of God dwell richly
In my heart from hour to hour,
So that all may see I triumph
Only through His power.

3   May the peace of God my Father
Rule my life in everything,
That I may be calm to comfort
Sick and sorrowing.

4   May the love of Jesus fill me,
As the waters fill the sea;
Him exalting, self abasing,
This is victory.

5   May I run the race before me,
Strong and brave to face the foe,
Looking only unto Jesus
As I onward go.

Kate B. Wilkinson

93

English Traditional Melody

1   Thine for ever! God of love,
      Hear us from Thy throne above;
      Thine for ever may we be,
      Here and in eternity.

2   Thine for ever! Lord of life,
      Shield us through our earthly strife:
      Thou the Life, the Truth, the Way,
      Guide us to the realms of day.

3   Thine for ever! O how blest
      They who find in Thee their rest!
      Saviour, Guardian, Heavenly Friend,
      O defend us to the end!

4   Thine for ever! Shepherd keep
      These Thy frail and trembling sheep;
      Safe alone beneath Thy care,
      Let us all Thy goodness share.

5   Thine for ever! Thou our guide,
      All our wants by Thee supplied,
      All our sins by Thee forgiven,
      Lead us, Lord, from earth to heaven.

Mary Fawler Maude

94

TUDOR C.M.

J. P. Jewson

1   Lord, I would own Thy tender care,
     And all Thy love to me;
    The food I eat, the clothes I wear
     Are all bestowed by Thee.

2   'Tis Thou preservest me from death
     And dangers every hour;
    I cannot draw another breath
     Unless Thou give me power.

3   My health, and friends, and parents dear,
     To me by God are given;
    I have not any blessing here
     But what is sent from heaven.

4   Such goodness, Lord, and constant care
     A child can ne'er repay;
    But may it be my daily prayer
     To love Thee and obey.

Ann Taylor

95

GOSTERWOOD 76.76.D.   *English Traditional Melody*

In moderate time ♩ = 100

1   I love to hear the story
        Which angel voices tell,
    How once the King of Glory
        Came down on earth to dwell.
    I am both weak and sinful,
        But this I surely know:
    The Lord came down to save me,
        Because He loved me so.

2   I'm glad my blessèd Saviour
        Was once a child like me,
    To show how pure and holy
        His little ones might be;
    And if I try to follow
        His footsteps here below,
    He never will forsake me,
        Because He loves me so.

3   To sing His love and mercy
        My sweetest songs I'll raise;
    And though I cannot see Him,
        I know He hears my praise:
    For He has kindly promised
        That even I may go
    To sing among His angels,
        Because He loves me so.

Emily Huntington Miller

167

96

Plymouth Collection,
(U. S. A.) 1855

1   Heavenly Father, may Thy blessing
      Rest upon Thy children now,
 When in prayer Thy name we hallow,
      When in prayer to Thee we bow:
 In the wondrous story reading
      Of the Lord of truth and grace,
 May we see Thy love reflected
      In the light of His dear face.

2   May we learn from this great story
      All the arts of friendliness;
 Truthful speech and honest action,
      Courage, patience, steadfastness;
 How to master self and temper,
      How to make our conduct fair;
 When to speak and when be silent,
      When to do and when forbear.

3   May His spirit wise and holy
      With His gifts our spirits bless,
 Make us loving, joyous, peaceful,
      Rich in goodness, gentleness,
 Strong in self-control and faithful,
      Kind in thought and deed; for He
 Sayeth,"What ye do for others
      Ye are doing unto Me".

William Charter Piggott

97

QUEM PASTORES LAUDAVERE 888.7

Melody from a 14th-century German MS.

1   Jesus, good above all other,
    Gentle child of gentle mother,
    In a stable born our brother,
       Give us grace to persevere.

2   Jesus, cradled in a manger,
    For us facing every danger,
    Living as a homeless stranger,
       Make we Thee our King most dear.

3   Jesus, for Thy people dying,
    Risen Master, death defying,
    Lord in heaven, Thy grace supplying,
       Keep us to Thy presence near.

4   Jesus, who our sorrows bearest,
    All our thoughts and hopes Thou sharest,
    Thou to man the truth declarest;
       Help us all Thy truth to hear.

5   Lord, in all our doings guide us;
    Pride and hate shall ne'er divide us;
    We'll go on with Thee beside us,
       And with joy we'll persevere!

Percy Dearmer

98

DUKE STREET L.M.

John Hatton, died 1793

1   Fight the good fight with all thy might,
    Christ is thy strength, and Christ thy right;
    Lay hold on life, and it shall be
    Thy joy and crown eternally.

2   Run the straight race through God's good grace,
    Lift up thine eyes, and seek His face;
    Life with its path before us lies,
    Christ is the way, and Christ the prize.

3   Cast care aside; lean on thy guide.
    His boundless mercy will provide;
    Trust, and thy trusting soul shall prove
    Christ is its life, and Christ its love.

4   Faint not, nor fear; His arm is near;
    He changeth not, and thou art dear;
    Only believe, and thou shalt see
    That Christ is all in all to thee.

                                    J. S. B. Monsell

99

MORNING LIGHT   76. 76. D   *G. J. Webb, 1803-87*

1   Stand up ! stand up for Jesus !
      Ye soldiers of the cross,
    Lift high His royal banner,
      It must not suffer loss.
    From victory unto victory
      His army shall He lead,
    Till every foe is vanquished,
      And Christ is Lord indeed.

2   Stand up! stand up for Jesus !
      The trumpet - call obey;
    Forth to the mighty conflict
      In this His glorious day.
    Ye that are men, now serve Him
      Against unnumbered foes;
    Let courage rise with danger,
      And strength to strength oppose.

3   Stand up! stand up for Jesus !
      Stand in His strength alone;
    The arm of flesh will fail you,
      Ye dare not trust your own.
    Put on the gospel armour,
      Each piece put on with prayer,
    Where duty calls, or danger,
      Be never wanting there.

4   Stand up! stand up for Jesus !
      The strife will not be long;
    This day the noise of battle,
      The next the victor's song.
    To him that overcometh
      A crown of life shall be;
    He with the King of glory
      Shall reign eternally.

George Duffield

100

JUST AS I AM 888.6   *Joseph Barnby, 1838-96*

1   Just as I am, Thine own to be,
    Friend of the young, who lovest me,
    To consecrate myself to Thee,
      O Jesus Christ, I come.

2   In the glad morning of my day,
    My life to give, my vows to pay,
    With no reserve and no delay,
      With all my heart I come.

3   I would live ever in the light,
    I would work ever for the right,
    I would serve Thee with all my might,
      Therefore to Thee I come.

4   Just as I am, young, strong and free
    To be the best that I can be
    For truth, and righteousness, and Thee,
      Lord of my life, I come.

Marianne Farningham

101

SHIPSTON 87.87

English Traditional Melody

1   Saviour, while my heart is tender,
      I would yield that heart to Thee,
   All my powers to Thee surrender,
      Thine, and only Thine, to be.

2   Take me now, Lord Jesus, take me;
      Let my youthful heart be Thine:
   Thy devoted servant make me;
      Fill my soul with love divine.

3   Send me, Lord, where Thou wilt send me,
      Only do Thou guide my way;
   May Thy grace through life attend me,
      Gladly then shall I obey.

4   Let me do Thy will or bear it;
      I would know no will but Thine:
   Shouldst Thou take my life or spare it,
      I that life to Thee resign.

5   Thine I am. O Lord, for ever,
      To Thy service set apart;
   Suffer me to leave Thee never;
      Seal Thine image on my heart.

John Burton

102

Melody in Corner's Gesangbuch, 1631
Arr. by W. S. Rockstro, 1823-95

1   Jesus calls us! O'er the tumult
       Of our life's wild restless sea
    Day by day His sweet voice soundeth,
       Saying: Christian, follow Me —

2   As of old, apostles heard it
       By the Galilean lake,
    Turned from home and toil and kindred,
       Leaving all for His dear sake.

3   Jesus calls us from the worship
       Of the vain world's golden store,
    From each idol that would keep us,
       Saying: Christian, love Me more.

4   In our joys and in our sorrows,
       Days of toil and hours of ease,
    Still He calls, in cares and pleasures,
       That we love Him more than these.

5   Jesus calls us! By Thy mercies,
       Saviour, make us hear Thy call,
    Give our hearts to Thine obedience,
       Serve and love Thee best of all.

                        Cecil Frances Alexander

103

CRÜGER 76.76.D

Adapted by W. H. Monk. 1823-89
from a chorale by J. Crüger, 1598-1662

1 O Jesus, I have promised
   To serve Thee to the end;
Be Thou for ever near me,
   My Master and my Friend:
I shall not fear the battle
   If Thou art by my side,
Nor wander from the pathway
   If Thou wilt be my guide.

2 O let me feel Thee near me;
   The world is ever near;
I see the sights that dazzle,
   The tempting sounds I hear;
My foes are ever near me,
   Around me and within;
But, Jesus, draw Thou nearer,
   And shield my soul from sin.

3 O let me hear Thee speaking
   In accents clear and still,
Above the storms of passion,
   The murmurs of self-will;
O speak to reassure me,
   To chasten or control;
O speak, and make me listen,
   Thou Guardian of my soul.

4 O Jesus, Thou hast promised,
   To all who follow Thee,
That where Thou art in glory
   There shall Thy servant be;
And, Jesus, I have promised
   To serve Thee to the end:
O give me grace to follow,
   My Master and my Friend.

John Ernest Bode

104

GRENOBLE L.M.

Grenoble Church Melody

1   The Lord is King! I own His power,
    His right to rule each day and hour;
    I own His claim on heart and will,
    And His demands I would fulfil.

2   He claims my heart, to keep it clean
    From all defiling taint of sin;
    He claims my will, that I may prove
    How swift obedience answers love.

3   He claims my hand for active life
    In noble deeds and worthy strife;
    He claims my feet, that in His ways
    I may walk boldly all my days.

4   He claims my lips, that purest word
    In all my converse may be heard;
    My motives, passions, thoughts, that these,
    My inner life, my King may please.

5   He claims the brightness of my youth,
    My earnest strivings after truth,
    My joy, my toil, my craftsman's skill;
    All have their place, and serve His will.

6   O Lord my King, I turn to Thee;
    Thy loyal service makes me free;
    My daily task Thou shalt assign;
    For heart and will and life are Thine.

Darley Terry

105

LORD I WANT

American Negro Spiritual

Lord I want to be a Chris-tian In my
heart, in my heart, Lord I want to be a
Chris-tian In my heart. In my heart.
In my heart. Lord I

want to be a Chris-tian in my heart.

2 Lord, I want to be more loving
   In my heart, in my heart.

3 Lord, I want to be more holy
   In my heart, in my heart.

4 Lord, I want to be like Jesus
   In my heart, in my heart.

TELLING OTHERS

106

La Woon Hyung
Arr. by A. Ewart Rusbridge, 1917-

KOREA S.M.

ST. MICHAEL S.M.   *Genevan Psalter, 1551*

1 The Saviour's precious blood,
    Hath made all nations one.
  United let us praise this deed
    The Father's love hath done.

2 In this vast world of men,
    A world so full of sin,
  No other theme can be our prayer
    Than this - Thy kingdom come.

3 In this sad world of war,
    Can peace be ever found ?
  Unless the love of Christ prevail
    True peace will not abound.

4 The Master's new command
    Was - love each other well.
  O brothers, let us all unite
    To do His holy will.

Tr. William Scott and
Yung Oon Kim

107

GO TELL

American Negro Spiritual

Go, tell it on the moun - - tain,

O-ver the hills and eve - ry where, Go, tell it on the

Fine

moun - tain, That Je-sus Christ is a - born.

When I was a sin - ner I

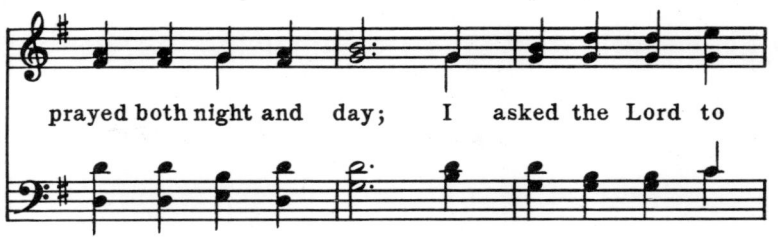

prayed both night and day; I asked the Lord to

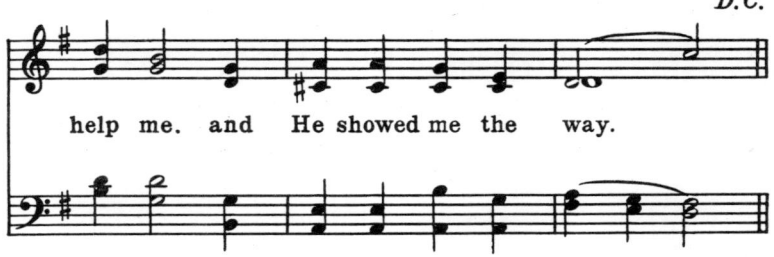

D.C.

help me. and He showed me the way.

2 When I was a seeker, I sought both night and day;
   I asked the Lord to help me, and He taught me to pray.

3 He made me a watchman upon the city wall;
   And if I am a Christian, I am the least of all.

108

JESUS SAVES **7. 3. 7. 3. 7. 7. 7. 3.**   *W. J. Kirkpatrick, 1838-1921*

1   We have heard a joyful sound:
       Jesus saves!
   Spread the gladness all around:
       Jesus saves!
   Bear the news to every land,
   Climb the steeps and cross the waves;
   Onward! 'tis our Lord's command:
       Jesus saves!

2   Sing above the battle's strife;
       Jesus saves!
   By His death and endless life,
       Jesus saves!
   Sing it softly through the gloom,
   When the heart for mercy craves;
   Sing in triumph o'er the tomb:
       Jesus saves!

3   Give the winds a mighty voice:
       Jesus saves!
   Let the nations now rejoice:
       Jesus saves!
   Sing ye islands of the sea;
   Echo back, ye ocean caves;
   Shout salvation full and free
       Jesus saves!

Priscilla Jane Owens

109

BREAD IN THE WILDERNESS   *Ewald J. Bash*

Very freely

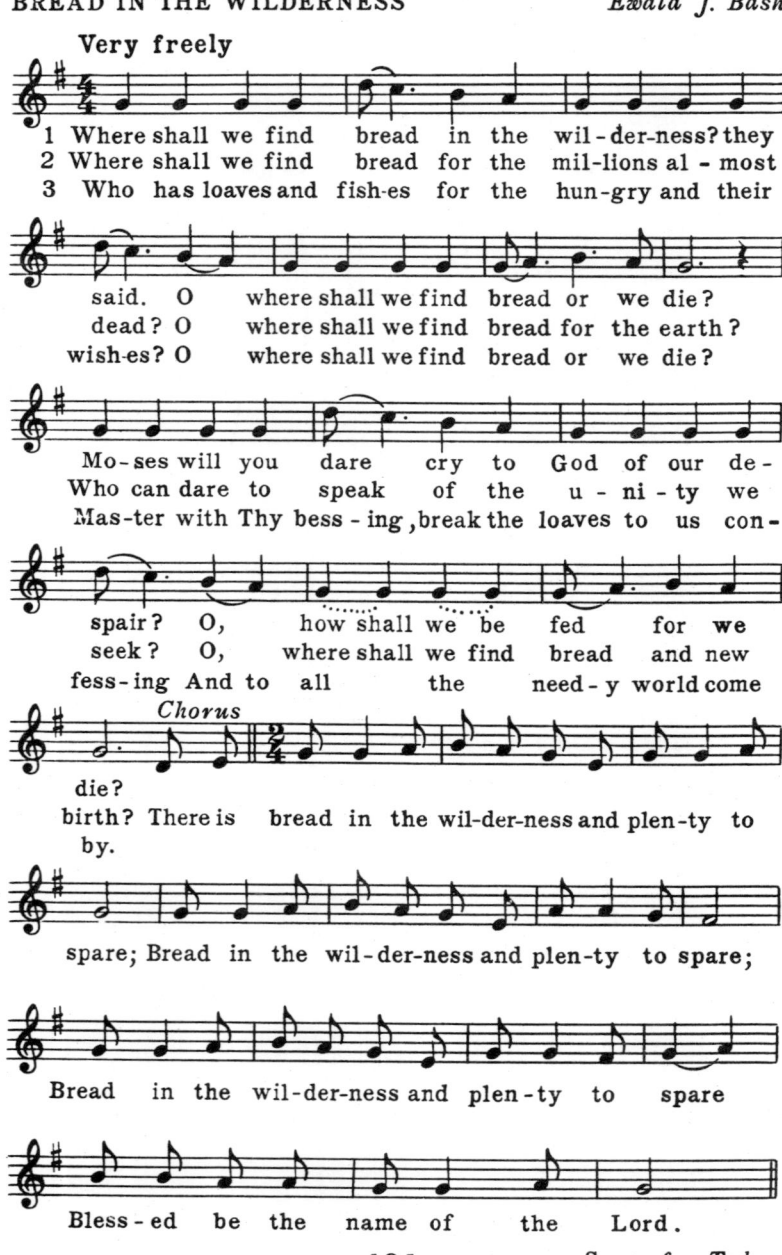

1 Where shall we find   bread   in   the   wil-der-ness? they
2 Where shall we find   bread   for   the   mil-lions al - most
3 Who has loaves and fish-es   for   the   hun-gry and their

said.   O   where shall we find   bread or   we die?
dead? O   where shall we find   bread for   the earth?
wish-es? O   where shall we find   bread or   we die?

Mo-ses will you   dare   cry   to   God   of our   de-
Who can dare to   speak   of the   u - ni - ty   we
Mas-ter with Thy bess - ing, break the loaves to   us   con-

spair?   O,   how shall we be   fed   for   we
seek?   O,   where shall we find   bread   and new
fess-ing And to   all   the   need - y world come

Chorus

die?
birth? There is   bread   in   the   wil-der-ness and plen-ty to
by.

spare; Bread   in   the   wil-der-ness and plen-ty to spare;

Bread   in   the   wil-der-ness and plen-ty   to   spare

Bless-ed   be   the   name   of   the   Lord.

Songs for Today

SPECIAL OCCASIONS
Morning and Evening

110

THANK YOU   *Martin G. Schneider*

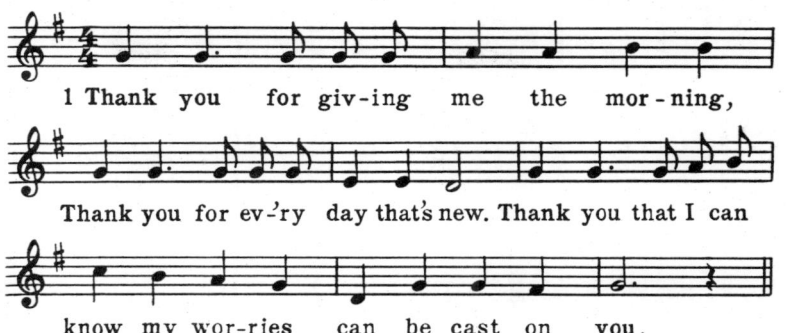

1 Thank you for giv-ing me the mor-ning,
Thank you for ev-'ry day that's new. Thank you that I can
know my wor-ries can be cast on you.

2   Thank you for all my friends and brothers,
Thank you for all the men that live,
Thank you for even greatest enemies
    I can forgive.

3   Thank you, I have my occupation,
Thank you for every pleasure small,
Thank you for music, light and gladness,
    thank you for them all.

4   Thank you for many little sorrows,
Thank you for every kindly word,
Thank you that everywhare your guidance
    reaches every land.

5   Thank you, I see your word has meaning,
Thank you, I know your sprit here,
Thank you because you love all people
    those both far and near.

6   Thank you, O Lord, you spoke unto us,
Thank you that for our words you care
Thank you, O Lord, you came among us,
    Bread and Wine to share.

7   Thank you, O Lord your love is boundless,
Thank you that I am full of you,
Thank you, you made me feel so glad and
    thankful as I do.

Walter Van der Haas and Others

111

ST. TIMOTHY C.M.

H.W. Baker, 1821-77

1 My Father, for another night
    Of quiet sleep and rest,
For all the joy of morning light
    Thy holy name be blest.

2 Now with the new-born day I give
    Myself anew to Thee,
That as Thou willest I may live,
    And what Thou willest be.

3 Whate'er I do, things great or small,
    Whate'er I speak or frame,
Thy glory may I seek in all,
    Do all in Jesu's name.

4 My Father, for His sake, I pray,
    Thy child accept and bless;
And lead me by Thy grace to-day
    In paths of righteousness.

Henry Williams Baker

112

SOLOTHURN L.M.   *Swiss Traditional Melody*

1   Father, we thank Thee for the night,
      And for the pleasant morning light;
      For rest and food and loving care,
      And all that makes the day so fair.

2   Help us to do the things we should,
      To be to others kind and good;
      In all we do at work or play
      To grow more loving every day.

Rebecca J. Weston

113

EUDOXIA 65.65.   *S. Baring-Gould, 1834-1924*

A-men.

1   Now the day is over,
        Night is drawing nigh,
    Shadows of the evening
        Steal across the sky.

2   Now the darkness gathers,
        Stars their watches keep,
    Birds and beasts and flowers
        Soon will be asleep.

3   Jesus, give the weary
        Calm and sweet repose;
    With Thy tenderest blessing
        May their eyelids close.

4   When the morning wakens,
        Then may I arise
    Pure, and fresh, and sinless
        In Thy holy eyes.

5   Glory to the Father,
        Glory to the Son,
    And to Thee, blest Spirit,
        Whilst all ages run.

S. Baring - Gould

114

LES COMMANDEMENS DE DIEU   *Adapted by L. Bourgeois*
98.98   *Genevan Psalter, 1543*

ST. CLEMENT 98.98   *C. C. Scholefield, 1839-1904*

1   The day Thou gavest, Lord, is ended,
    The darkness falls at Thy behest;
    To Thee our morning hyms ascended,
    Thy praise shall hallow now our rest.

2   We thank Thee that Thy Church unsleeping
    While earth rolls onward into light,
    Through all the world her watch is keeping
    And rests not now by day or night.

3   As o'er each continent and island
    The dawn leads on another day,
    The voice of prayer is never silent,
    Nor dies the strain of praise away.

4   The sun, that bids us rest, is waking
    Our brethren neath the western sky,
    And hour by hour fresh lips are making
    Thy wondrous doings heard on high.

5   So be it, Lord; Thy throne shall never,
    Like earth's proud empires, pass away;
    But stand, and rule, and grow for ever,
    Till all Thy creatures own Thy sway.

John Ellerton

115

THIS IS SUNDAY

O. A. Boateng

1 This is Sunday, the day God has blessed!
Work on other days - on Sunday you must rest;
    So we do no work today,
    But we come to church and say,
"Sunday brings us blessing,
Sunday brings us blessing, blessing, blessing!"

2 Let us all read the Bible today!
What we read we must endeavour to obey;
    For it speaks to me and you,
    And it tells us what to do.
Sunday brings us blessing,
Sunday brings us blessing, blessing, blessing!

3 Jesus calls, "Boys and girls, gather round!"
When we sing, the Saviour loves to hear the sound;
    So we praise His holy name;
    'Twas for us that Jesus came.
Sunday brings us blessing,
Sunday brings us blessing, blessing, blessing!

Tr. by P. Barker

116

AURELIA 76. 76. D

S. S. Wesley, 1810-76

1   O day of rest and gladness,
     O day of joy and light,
  O balm of care and sadness,
     Most beautiful, most bright!
  On thee the high and lowly,
     Through ages joined in tune,
  Sing, "Holy, holy, holy,"
     To the great God triune.

2   On thee, at the creation,
     The light first had its birth;
  On thee, for our salvation,
     Christ rose from depths of earth;
  On thee our Lord victorious
     The Spirit sent from heaven:
  And thus on thee most glorious
     A triple light was given.

3   New graces ever gaining
     From this our day of rest,
  We reach the rest remaining
     To spirits of the blest,
  To Holy Ghost be praises,
     To Father and to Son;
  The Church her voice upraises
     To Thee, blest Three in One.

Christopher Wordsworth, altd.

NEW YEAR AND THE SEASONS

117

NOT IMPOSSIBLE FOR GOD   *Prof. Chas E. Graves*

1 When we sowed the corn and we dug the farm
  We could not be sure that the rain would come,
  But we trusted God, because we knew
  It was not impossible for Him to do.

        Chorus: Let the heavens sing,
                Let the earth join in,
                Crying out with one accord to praise the King !
                By the old and young
                Let the song be sung,
                Men and women join to praise the Holy One !

2 So long as sun and rain are there
  There'll be food enough for us to share,
  For our God has got us in his care –
  It is not impossible for Him to do.

3 O Master, who our fathers led,
  We rely on you for daily bread;
  And whate'er we face in the days ahead,
  It is not impossible for you to do.

Tr. by P. Barker

118

CHERRY TREE CAROL *Traditional English Carol Melody*
7.6.7.6.

1 Another year is dawning:
   Dear Master, let it be,
In working or in waiting,
   Another year for Thee:

2 Another year of mercies,
   Of faithfulness and grace;
Another year of gladness
   In the shining of Thy face:

3 Another year of progress,
   Another year of praise,
Another year of proving
   Thy presence all the days:

4 Another year of service,
   Of witness for Thy love;
Another year of training
   For holier work above.

5 Another year is dawning:
   Dear Master, let it be,
On earth, or else in heaven,
   Another year for Thee.

Frances Ridley Havergal

119

DISMISSAL 87. 87. 87   *W. L. Viner, 1790-1867*

1   Lord, behold us with Thy blessing
        Once again assembled here;
    Onward be our footsteps pressing,
        In Thy love, and faith, and fear;
    Still protect us, still protect us
    By Thy presence ever near.

2   For Thy mercy we adore Thee,
        For this rest upon our way;
    Lord, again we bow before Thee,
        Speed our labours day by day;
    Mind and spirit, mind and spirit
    With Thy choicest gifts array.

3   Keep the spell of home affection
        Still alive in every heart;
    May its power, with mild direction,
        Draw our love from self apart,
    Till Thy children, till Thy chilren
    Feel that Thou their Father art.

                    Henry James Buckoll

120

RHUDDLAN 87. 87. 87

Welsh Traditional Melody

1   Lord, dismiss us with Thy blessing,
    Thanks for mercies past receive;
    Pardon all, their faults confessing;
    Time that's lost may all retrieve;
      May Thy children, may Thy children
    Ne'er again Thy Spirit grieve.

2   By Thy kindly influence cherish
    All the good we here have gained;
    May all taint of evil perish,
    By Thy mightier power restrained;
      Seek we ever, seek we ever
    Knowledge pure and love unfeigned.

3   Let Thy Father-hand be shielding
    All who here shall meet no more;
    May their seed-time past be yielding
    Year by year a richer store;
      Those returning, those returning
    Make more faithful than before.

Henry James Buckoll

121

RANDOLPH 98.89   R. Vaughan Willams, 1872 - 1958

Unison   Harmony

Unison

1 God be with you till we meet again;
      May He through the days direct you;
      May He in life's storms protect you;
   God be with you till we meet again.

2 God be with you till we meet again;
      And when doubts and fears oppress you;
      May His holy peace possess you;
   God be with you till we meet again.

3 God be with you till we meet again;
      In distress His grace sustain you;
      In success from pride restrain you;
   God be with you till we meet again.

4 God be with you till we meet again;
      May He go through life beside you;
      And through death in safety guide you;
   God be with you till we meet again.

D. W. Hughes

CARE FOR THE ILL OR NEEDY

122

FERRY C.M.

Green's Psalmody, 1731

1 Father, whose will is life and good
     For all of mortal breath,
   Bind strong the bond of brotherhood
     Of those who fight with death.

2 Empower the hands and hearts and wills
     Of friends in lands afar,
   Who battle with the body's ills,
     And wage Thy holy war.

3 Where'er they heal the maimed and blind,
     Let love of Christ attend,
   Proclaim the good Physician's mind,
     And prove the Saviour friend.

4 For Christ the Lord can now employ
     As agents of His will,
   Restoring strength and health and joy,
     The doctor's love and skill.

5 O Father, look from heaven and bless,
     Where'er Thy servants be,
   Their works of pure unselfishness,
     Made consecrate to Thee!

H. D. Rawnsley, altd.

123

GOD BLESS AFRICA

Bless O Lord our land of A - fri - ca

Lift its name and make its peo - ple free,

Take the gifts we o - ffer un - to Thee, Hear us

faith - ful sons, hear us faith - ful sons.

124

KINGSFOLD D.C.M.   *from an English Traditional Melody*

1   O God of love, whose spirit wakes
        In every human breast,
    Whom love, and love alone, can know,
        In whom all hearts find rest.
    Help us to spread Thy gracious reign,
        Till greed and hate shall cease,
    And kindness dwell in human hearts,
        And all the earth find peace.

2   O God of truth, whom science seeks
        And reverent souls adore,
    Who lightest every earnest mind
        Of every clime and shore,
    Dispel the gloom of error's night;
        Of ignorance and fear,
    Until true wisdom from above
        Shall make life's pathway clear.

3   O God of beauty, oft revealed
        In dreams of human art,
    In speech that flows to melody,
        In holiness of heart;
    Teach us to ban all ugliness
        That blinds our eyes to Thee,
    Till all shall know the loveliness
        Of lives made fair and free.

4   O God of righteousness and grace,
        Seen in the Christ, Thy Son,
    Whose life and death reveal Thy face,
        By whom Thy will was done,
    Inspire Thy heralds of good news
        To live Thy life divine,
    Till Christ is formed in all mankind,
        And every land is Thine.

H. H. Tweedy

125

ST. STEPHEN C.M. *William Jones, 1726-1800*

1 In Christ there is no East or West,
   In Him no South or North,
   But one great fellowship of love
   Throughout the whole wide earth.

2 In Him shall true hearts everywhere
   Their high communion find:
   His service is the golden cord
   Close - binding all mankind.

3 Join hands then, brothers of the faith,
   Whate'er your race may be !
   Who serves my Father as a son
   Is surely kin to me.

4 In Christ now meet both East and West,
   In Him meet South and North,
   All Christly souls are one in Him,
   Throughout the whole wide earth.

John Oxenham

126

LORD HAVE MERCY

Missa Mikaeli Mtakatifu
David Powell (adapted)

In free rhythm
Sing 3 times
Leader   *Chorus*

Lord,_____ have mer-cy u-pon us,

Sing 3 times
Leader   *Chorus*

Christ, _____ have mer - cy u - pon us,

Sing 3 times
Leader   *Chorus*

Lord,_____ have mer-cy u-pon us.

127

HOLY, HOLY, HOLY   Irregular

Missa Malawi (adapted)
Victor Mwachumo Chunga

Ho - ly, Ho - ly,_____ Ho -
ly,_____ Lord God of Hosts, Hea-ven and
earth are__ full of thy glo - -
ry, Ho - sa - na,_____ in the high - est.__

128

LAMB OF GOD

Miles Manyawu

Slowly

Lamb of __ God, who ta - - kest a way the sins of the world, have mer - cy u - pon us;

3rd time world, grant us __ peace. __

129

LAUDAMUS   *from the Zulu Church*

Save us dear Lord, bless your he - ri-tage;

Gov-ern us with love, and lift us up for - e -ver.

We mag - ni - fy you day by day dear, Lord;

Now and e - ver we wor - ship your name.

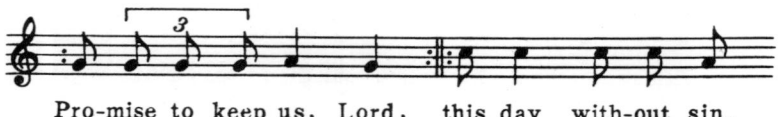

Pro-mise to keep us, Lord, this day with-out sin.

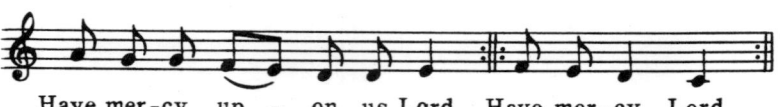

Have mer-cy up - on us Lord. Have mer-cy Lord.

As we have trust in you, on - ly you,

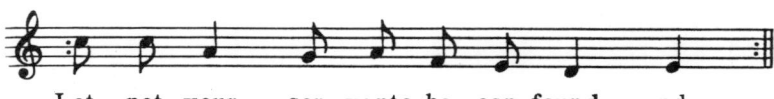

Let not your ser - vants be con - found - ed.

E - ver___ more we wor - ship you.

E - ver more we mag - ni - fy you;

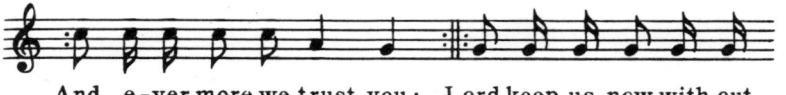

And e - ver more we trust you; Lord keep us now with-out

sin, Have mer-cy on us. Save your peo-ple O Lord,

E - ver bless your he - ri - tage. A_____ men.

From the Te Deum

HYMNS

TUNES SET IN
TONIC SOL FA

GOD OUR FATHER

1

O PRAISE THE KING   *Wedding Song, Malawi*

Doh is **F**

Leader   *In the Chorus, the tune is in the middle part*

O praise the King of hea - - ven,   O praise the King of

```
{ :l | l  :— :l | l :— :l | l  :— :— | m :— :l | l  :— :l | l :— :l }
{ [:r | r  :— :r | r :— :r | r  :— :— | l, :— :r | r  :— :r | r :— :r }
```

hea - ven   all ye   who are   his peo - ple.

```
{ | l  :— :s | — :— :m | s  :— :m | s :— :m | r :— :d | — :— ||
{ | r  :— :d | — :— :d | d  :— :d | d :— :d | l, :— :s, | — :— ] ||
```

Chorus   Ye prin - - ces!

```
{ :       |    : :s | s :— :s | l :— :s |  : :s | m :— :— | d :— :— }
{ O     | praise the King of | hea - ven,       |        O }
{ :s    | s  :— :m | m :— :m | r :— :d | — :— : |  : : |  : :s }
{ :d    | d  :— :d | d :— :d | l, :— :s, | — :— : |  : : |  : :d }
```

```
{        :  :s | s :— :s | l :— :s | — :— :s | s :— :s | l :— :l }
{ praise the King of | hea - ven,      the | ho - ly gra - cious }
{ s  :— :m | m :— :m | r :— :d | — :— :m | m :— :m | r :— :d }
{ d  :— :d | d :— :d | l, :— :s, | — :— :d | d :— :d | l, :— :l, }
```

                     Ye ru - - lers!

```
{ l  :— :— | — :— :s | m :— :— | d :— :— |   : :s | s :— :s }
{ King!              |        O | praise the King of }
{ l, :— :— | — :— :  |  : : |  : :s | s :— :m | m :— :m }
{ l, :— :— | — :— :  |  : : |  : :d | d :— :d | d :— :d }
```

                     Ale - lu - - ya!

```
{ l  :— :s | — :— :s .s | s :— :— | m :— :— |   : :s | s :— :s }
{ hea - ven,            |        O | praise the King of }
{ r  :— :d |  : : . |  : : |  : :s | s :— :m | m :— :m }
{ l, :— :s, |  : : . |  : : |  : :d | d :— :d | d :— :d }
```

```
| 1  :— :s |— :— :s | s  :— :s |1 :— :1 | 1  :— :— |— :—  ‖
|hea - ven,     the |ho - ly gra - cious|King!              ‖
| r  :— :d |— :— :m | m  :— :m |r  :— :d | 1, :— :— |— :—  ‖
| 1, :— :s, |— :— :d | d  :— :d |1, :— :1, | 1, :— :— |— :—  ‖
```

2 L: O tell abroad His glory,
      O tell abroad His glory,
      And publish it to all men.
      Ye fathers! Ye mothers! Aleluya!

  C: *O praise the King of heaven, etc.*

3 L: O shout aloud His praises,
      O shout aloud His praises
      In mountain, plain and valley.
      Young warriors! Ye maidens! Aleluya!

  C: *O praise the King of heaven, etc.*

4 L: For He is high exalted,
      For He is high exalted
      Above all earthly nations.
      Old people! Ye children! Aleluya!

  C: *O praise the King of heaven, etc.*

5 L: For God, the great God reigneth,
      For God, the great God reigneth
      Above all tribes and peoples.
      In heaven! On earth! Aleluya!

  C: *O praise the King of heaven, etc.*

Mawelera Tembo

2

LET THE WORLD   *Malawi Melody*

Doh is G

Let	the	world	in	con - cert	sing
s	:m .r	ld	:d	l :l	ls :—
:		ls .m	:s .m	lr :r	ls, :—
		Let	the world in	con - cert	sing

Prai - ses	to	our	glor - ious	King:
s	:m .r	ld	:d	l :l	ls :—
:		ls .m	:s .m	lr :r	ls, :—
		Prai - ses	to our	glor - ious	King:

A	-	le - lu	-	ya,	A	-	le -
s	:— .s	l1	:—	s	:—	ls	:— .s
m	:— .m	lr	:—	s,	:—	lm	:— .m

lu	-	ya		to	our	King!
l	:—	ls	:—	s	:fe	ls :—
r	:—	ls,	:—	d	:l,	ls, :—

2 Of His power and glory tell:
All His work He doeth well:
Aleluya, aleluya to our King!

3 Come, behold what He hath done,
Deeds of wonder every one:
Aleluya, aleluya to our King!

4 O ye fearful ones, draw near:
Praise our God who holds you dear:
Aleluya, aleluya to our King!

5 Let us now in concert sing
Praises to our glorious King:
Aleluya, aleluya to our King!

Mawelera Tembo

3

LET US PRAISE THE LORD   *Abraham Maraire*

Doh is C
Fast

Leader

S	d' .d' :d' .d' :d' .d'	l .l :— :— ‖
	Let us praise the Lord our Ma-ker	
	[*Chorus*] : :	:d' .d' :l
	For all the
T	: :	:d' .d' :l
B	d :s :d	f :— :—
	Praise Him, praise Him,

d' :d' :t	s .s :— .s :m ‖
good things He's	gi - ven to us
d' :d' :t	s .s :— .s :m
d :d :m	s .s :— .s :m
good things He's	gi - ven to us

Verse 1
Leader

d' .d' :d' .d' :s	l :— :— ‖
For He gives us our	food
: :	:d' .d' :d' .l
And He gives us
: :	:d' .d' :d' .l
d :s :d	f :— :—
Praise Him, praise	Him,

d' :d' :t	s .s :s .s :m ‖
good things to	bless us all our lives.
d' :d' :t	s .s :s .s :m
d :d :m	s .s :s .s :m
good things to	bless us all our lives.

234

Keep on as above, except that the leader sings:

{| d' .d' :d' .s :l̄ | l :— :— ‖

And He gives us wa - ter.
And He gives us sun - shine.
And He gives us bree - zes.　　　*Repeat Chorus*

Sing as in Verse 1
Verse 2
Leder

{| d' .d' :d' .d' :d' .d' | l :— :— ‖

For He gives us dai - ly work

{| d' .d' :d' .d' :s̄ | l :— :— ‖

And He gives us mo - ney
And He gives us know - ledge

{|s .d' :d' .d' :d' .d' | l :l :— ‖

So our lives are tru - ly ble - ssed.
　　　Repeat Chorus

Verse 3

{| d' .d' :d' .d' :d̄' | l :— :— ‖

He gave us our par - ents

{| d' .d' :d' .d' :d' .s | l :— :— ‖

And He gives us ma - ny friends

{| d' .d' :d' .s :l̄ .l | l :— :— ‖

He gives us our fa - mi - lies

{| d .d :d .d :s̄ | l :— :— ‖

And He gives us chil - dren
　　　Repeat Chorus

235

4

GOD OUR FATHER WE BESEECH THEE *Abraham Maraire*

Doh is G

Chorus

Drum

```
      :x :  :  :  :         :x  :    :    :     :
Leader
d  :f :l  :l, :d  :— .s, | t,   :s,  :    :    :     :
God our Fa-ther, we    be-se ech Thee
T  d  :f :— :— :m :— .d | m   :r  :    :    :     :
Fa-ther,        we    be-seach Thee, Look on us Thy child-ren.
B  d, :f, :— :— :m, :— .d, | m,  :s,  :d  .d :d .s, :l, .l, :—
```

Verses

Drum

```
      :x        :        :    :   :        :x :  :  :  :
Leader
d  :f  .f :f  .f :l,   :d :— .s, | t,  :s, :  :  :  :
A - bide with  me  in  my  dai - ly la-bour
Con-tin - ue with  me through all    my life-time.
```

Repeat Chorus after each Verse

Verse 4 line 3

```
{| d   :f .f :f .f :f  .l, :d :— .s, | t,  :s, :  :  :  :
Where people are in trou-ble please    a-ssist them.
```

2   The Lord takes care of us when we're sleeping
    The Lord takes care of us when we're walking
    The Lord takes care of us when we're working
    The Lord takes care of us in our lessons.

3   Wherever I may go be my refuge
    Wherever they may be watch my family
    Wherever they may be watch my friends too.

4   Watch over people throughout the whole world
    Where people still are ill heal their sickness
    Where people are in trouble please assist them
    Beneath Thy wings we find strength and refuge.

6

LET US PRAISE THE CREATOR   *From a hunting song*

Doh is G

Quite fast

(1) *Drum*

The tonic sol-fa notation with parts:

Drum: d :s₁ :d :d :d :d̄ :d̄ :d̄ | d :s₁ :d :d :d :d̄ :d̄ :d̄

Rattle: ✕ : :✕ :✕ : :✕ :✕ : | ✕ : :✕ :✕ : :✕ :✕ :

Leader: f .f :m .m |(m) .f :r | d : | :

Let us praise the—Cre-a - tor

S: | f f :m .m |(m) .r :d

Let us praise the—Cre-a -

B: f₁ :l₁ |— :r₁ | f₁ :l₁ |— :d₁

0, ———— 0, ———— 0, ——

---

d :s₁ :d :d :d :d̄ :d̄ :d̄ | d :s₁ :d :d :d :d̄ :d̄ :d̄

✕ : :✕ :✕ : :✕ :✕ : | ✕ : :✕ :✕ : :✕ :✕ :

m :r .r |(r) .m :d | t₁ :l₁ .l₁ |l₁ .d :d

Who loves all—His child - ren, Praise the Lord of Hosts.

t₁ (2) :s₁ .s₁ |— .s₁ :d₁ | m₁ :l₁ .l₁ |l₁ .d :d

tor, Praise to the Lord Oh, praise the Lord of Hosts.

m₁ :s₁ |— :d₁ | m₁ :l₁ .l₁ |l₁ .f₁ :f₁

0, ———— Praise the Lord of Hosts.

---

(1) The drum has two pitches high and low: *Doh* and *Soh* are used merely to indicate this.

(2) All verses. (Trebles sing only the first line of each verse).

2 It is He who gives us water
   In the fields where we labour;
   Praise the Lord of Hosts.

3 It is He who gives us wisdom
   To do the things we ought to;
   Praise the Lord of Hosts.

4 It is He who gave us Jesus
   To save us from all evil;
   Praise the Lord of Hosts.

5 If we give ourselves to Jesus
   Then we will lack for nothing;
   Praise the Lord of Hosts.

6 O, lead us, our Father
   To be with Thee forever;
   Praise the Lord of Hosts.

*Note.   The basses sing "O" during the first two lines of each
   verse.   Trebles sing the first line of each verse and then:
   "Praise to the Lord, O praise the Lord of Hosts."*

7

JOYFUL TIDING   *Kikongo Melody*

Doh is G
[*Introduction*]

Leader

{| d :— :d |m :— :r | d :— :— |d :— :d }
O   what joy - ful   ti   -   dings great

{| d :— :m |s :— :l |r :— :— |— :— :— |— :— :r }
ha - ppi-ness   is ours   Re -

{| s :s :s |s :s :s | s :s :s |m :m :r }
joice and be glad for the   Sa-viour has come to the

                                              Chorus
{| m :— :r |d :— :— | — :— :d |m :— :r ‖
earth   from God   What joy - ful

%
{| d :— :— |d :— :d | d :— :m |s :— :l }
ti -   dings,   great ha - ppi-ness   is

{| r :— :— |— :— :— |— :— :r | s :s :s |s :s :s }
ours,   Re - joice and be glad for the

{| s :s :s |m :m :r | m :— :r |d :— :— }
Sa-viour has come to   the earth   from God

                End. *Leader*
{| — :— :— ‖ m :— :f | s :— :— |s :— :— }
                Verse 1 With   won -   drous

{| s :— :— |m :— :f |s :— :— |l :— :— |r :— ‖
love   des - pite   our   sin,

240

Chorus

{| r | s :s :s | s :s :s | s :s :s | m :m :r }

Re - joice and be glad for the Sa-viour has come to the

Leader

{| m :— :r | d :— :— | — :— :— || m :— :f | s :— :— | s :— :— }

earth from God   He sought our

{| s :— :— | m :— :f | s :— :— | l :— :— | r :— || }

faith - less hearts to win,

Chorus

{| r | s :s :s | s :s :s | s :s :s | m :m :r }

Re-joice and be glad for the Sa-viour has come to the

Back to sign %

Chorus

{| m :— :r | d :— :— | — :— || d | m :— :r || }

earth from God   What joy - ful

2 All goodly things we see or know
     Rejoice and be glad ...
  From Him they come to men below.
     Rejoice and be glad ...

3 The love of God reigns all above
     Rejoice and be glad ...
  For men could not destroy His love.
     Rejoice and be glad ...

4 O Christ is King for evermore
     Rejoice and be glad ...
  Mankind in Him your God adore.
     Rejoice and be glad ...

(Repeat chorus after each verse)

Lucien Fwasi, tr. by A.S. Cox

12

GOD OUR FATHER   *Nsenga tune; Zambia*

Doh is D

Leader   *Chorus*

{ :d .r | m :m || l .l | s :s .m :s .m }

God our Fa - ther   So He loved the   whole

{| r :— :s .m | d :r .f :m .r | d :— ||

world   So He loved the   whole world.

In succeeding verses, repeat line 2 as above.

2 L: He sent Jesus
   C: *He sent Jesus to us*

3 L: He so loves us
   C: *That He died for us all*

4 L: He is risen
   C: *He is risen indeed*

5 L: He ascended
   C: *He ascended to His home*

6 L: Risen Jesus
   C: *Risen Jesus is King*

7 L: Loving Jesus
   C: *He is caring for all*

8 L: Jesus calls us
   C: *Jesus calls us today*

9 L: Let us hear Him
   C: *Let us hear His true Word*

10 L: Let us thank Him
   C: *For He gives us His life*

Nsenga hymn; tr. by Patrick Appleford and Francis Makambwe

JESUS CHRIST OUR LORD
His Birth

22

ON THE EVE

Bemba tune. Zambia

Doh is F

Brightly and **quickly**

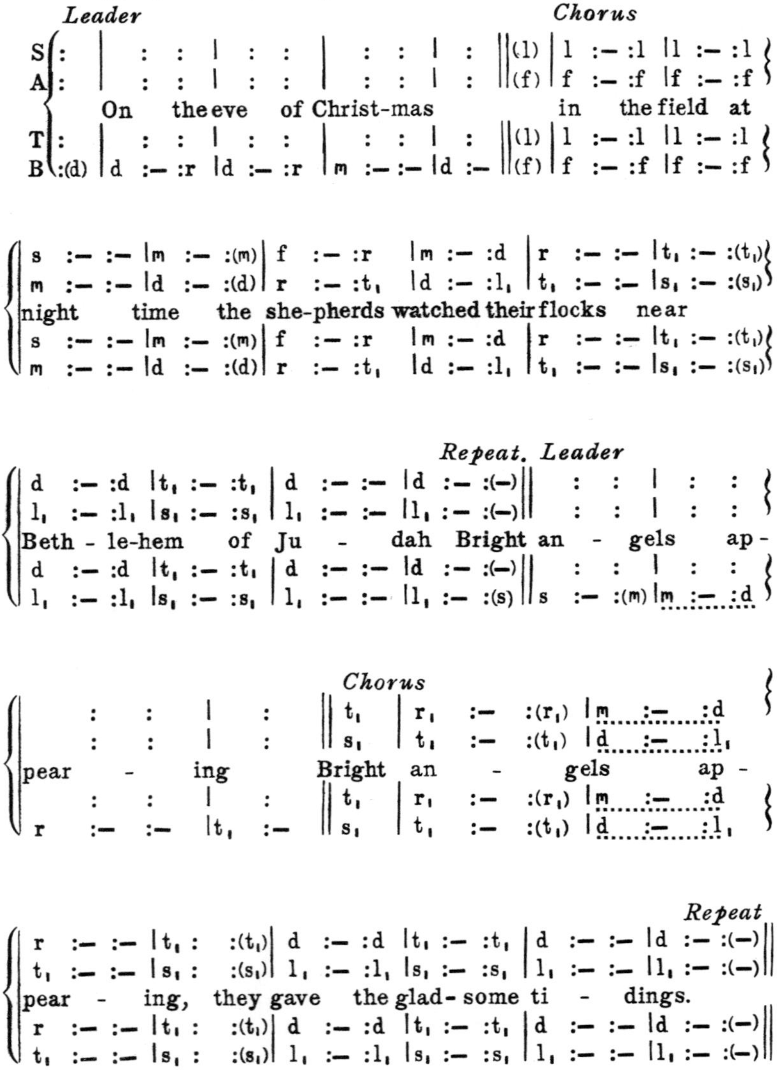

244

2 L: "Born is now the Baby,
   C: Christ, the world's Redeemer, } *Twice*
        God in flesh incarnate,
        lying in a manger:

   L: To Bethlehem go ye
       to Bethlehem go ye: } *Twice*
       there shall you behold Him."

3 L: "Mystery exceeding!
   C: Let us go to seek Him, } *Twice*
        to Bethlehem returning,
        as the angels told us.

   L: The Saviour, we seek Him,
       The Saviour, we seek Him: } *Twice*
       mystery exceeding!"

4 L: At the inn arriving
   C: amid the lowly cattle, } *Twice*
        they found Him in the stable
        with Mary and with Joseph.

   L: The Saviour they worshipped,
       The Saviour they worshipped, } *Twice*
       kneeling there before Him.

5 L: Now on this happy morning,
   C: O come let us adore Him, } *Twice*
        with heart and voice rejoicing
        to worship our Redeemer.

   L: O come let us adore Him,
   C: O come let us adore Him, } *Twice*
        Born for us at Christmas!

A. M. Jones

23

HE WAS BORN

Doh is G

```
⎧ m  :—.l |s  :m  | d  :r  |l₁ :—  | s₁ :d  |r  :m  | r  :—  |— :—  ⎫
⎪ d  :—.d |d  :d  | m₁ :l₁ |f₁ :—  | m₁ :s₁ |s₁ :s₁ | s₁ :—  |— :—  ⎪
⎨ s  :—.f |m  :s  | d  :f  |f  :—  | d  :m  |t₁ :d  | t₁ :—  |— :—  ⎬
⎩ d  :—.d |d  :d  | d  :f  |f₁ :—  | d  :d  |t₁ :d  | s₁ :—  |— :—  ⎭
```

```
⎧ m  :—.l |s  :m  | d  :r₁ |l₁ :—  | s₁ :d  |m  :r  | d  :—  |— :—  ⎫
⎪ d  :—.d |d  :d  | m₁ :l₁ |f₁ :—  | m₁ :m₁ |s₁ :s₁ | m₁ :—  |— :—  ⎪
⎨ s  :—.f |m  :s  | d  :f  |f  :—  | s₁ :s₁ |d  :t₁ | d  :—  |— :—  ⎬
⎩ d  :—.d |d  :d  | d  :f  |f₁ :—  | s₁ :s₁ |s₁ :s₁ | d₁ :—  |— :—  ⎭
```

```
⎧ s₁ :d  |r  :s  | m  :—  |d  :—  | s₁ :d  |r  :m  | r  :—  |— :—  ⎫
⎪ s₁ :d  |r  :s  | m  :—  |d  :—  | s₁ :d  |r  :m  | r  :—  |— :—  ⎪
⎨ m  :m  |r  :r  | m  :—  |m  :—  | m  :m  |t₁ :d  | t₁ :—  |— :—  ⎬
⎩ d  :d  |t₁ :t₁ | d  :—  |d  :—  | d  :d  |t₁ :d  | s₁ :—  |— :—  ⎭
```

```
⎧ m  :—.l |s  :m  | d  :r  |l₁ :—  | s₁ :d  |m  :r  | d  :—  |— :—  ⎫
⎪ d  :—.d |d  :d  | m₁ :l₁ |l₁ :—  | m₁ :m₁ |s₁ :f₁ | m₁ :—  |— :—  ⎪
⎨ s  :—.f |m  :s  | d  :f  |f  :—  | s₁ :s₁ |d  :t₁ | d  :—  |— :—  ⎬
⎩ d  :—.d |d  :d  | d  :f  |f₁ :—  | s₁ :s₁ |s₁ :s₁ | d₁ :—  |— :—  ⎭
```

1 He was born a little child when He came to earth:
Angels in the heavens above told us of His birth.

*Chorus: Mother Mary laid Him in a cattle stall,
        Little baby Jesus, who was Lord of all.*

2 Shepherds and their quiet sheep saw the angel bright:
Shepherds heard the angels singing in the night.

3 In the hills they left the lambs and the sleeping sheep:
Down to Bethlehem they came Jesus for to seek.

4 "Shepherds, whence your eager feet, running, running still ?
Who is caring for your sheep on the starlit hill ?"

5 "Shall we not adore Him, lying in the hay ?
Lo, our Saviour Jesus born to us to day!"

Tunes from Nyasaland

24

GOD THE FATHER

Doh is A   *The tune is in the middle part*

{ :m :— :m | r :— :— |d :— :— | — :— :— |m :— :m }
{ God   the | Fa -   ther, | from His }
{ :m :— :m | r :— :— |d :— :— | — :— :— |m :— :m }
{ :d :— :d | l₁ :— :— |m₁ :— :— | l₁ :— :— |m₁ :— :m₁ }

{ r :— :r |m :— :d | l₁ :— :— |m :— :m }
{ throne   in heaven   a - bove,   Sent   His }
{ r :— :r |m :— :d | l₁ :— :— |d :— :d }
{ l₁ :— :l₁ |m₁ :— :m₁ | r₁ :— :— |s₁ :— :s₁ }

{ m :— :— |m :— :— | m :— :r |d .— :— ‖ }
{ Son   to | us   in love }
{ d :— :— |d :— :— | d :— :l₁ |s₁ :— :— }
{ s₁ :— :— |s₁ :— :— | s₁ :— :r₁ |d₁ :— :— ‖ }

248

2 Lo, Lord Jesus, Jesus came a Saviour then,
Came to die for sinful men.

3 Heavenly angels sang in wonder at His birth,
"Christ the Saviour comes to earth!"

4 Aleluya, aleluya to our Lord!
Ever be His name adored!

5 For He bringeth, bringeth peace to all men,
Aleluya! Amen!

Elija Chavula

26

SONG OF JOSEPH

Abraham Maraire

Doh is E♭

Drum   :d

Wood block

S

T

B

"Ma - ry   please try   just   to
Ma - ry   please try   just   to
Ma - ry, when   will   we   be   a - ble to

Repeat

hur - ry   some   more.
hur - ry   some   more.
reach   Beth - le - hem?   Ma - ry,

See   all   the   peo - ple   who leave   us   be -
We   shall   not   find   room   to   stay   at   the
when   will   we   be   a - ble to reach Beth - le -

Repeat

hind,   Yet   I   can   see   that   the
inn,   And   al - so   tru - ly   the
hem?   Ma - ry, when   will   we   be   a - ble to

s₁	:—	s₁	:d	s₁	:—	s₁	:—	s₁	:s₁	d	:s₁	d	:—		:d
:	|×	:		:			:		:	|×	:		:			:
s₁	:—	s₁	:—	d	:—	m	:—	d	:—	:—		:—	:—		:—
child	does		make	you		tired
jour -	ney		is	too		long."
s	:—	:—	s	:—	:—	m	:—	s	:—	:—	l	:—	:—	l	:—
d	:—	:—	d	:—	:—	l₁	:—	d	:—	:—	d	:—	:—	m	:—
reach	Beth	-	le -	hem?		Ma	-		ry,

*The drum has two pitches, high and low: Doh and Soh have been used, not to show exact pitches, but to indicate which are high or low beats.

2 All of the people had left them behind,
  When they arrived it was already late.
  All of the houses were filled up with guests,
  But in the stable there was room for them.
  Yet they were troubled because of Mary's child,
  To sleep there that night, and yet they had no choice.

✶
Tenor & bass: God accompanied them while
              they were still on their way.

3 There in the stable that very same night
  The will of God was fulfilled here on earth.
  Then God did send a bright star as a sign
  To show to people that Jesus was King.
  Let there be peace among people here on earth,
  And also love in the hearts of all mankind.

Tenor & bass: Thus the will of the Father
              was fulfilled here on earth.

4 Let us now do as if in Bethlehem;
  Let us shout praises with hearts full of joy.
  A newborn baby is given to us;
  Let us thank God now for all He has done.
  Now let our hearts also be reborn with Him.
  So that we show gratitude and give Him praise.

Tenor & bass: Let us praise our Lord God
              for all the things He has done,
              Let us share with one
              another in true Christian love.

*The tenors and basses keep on repeating their words.
In each verse (except verse 4) they sing their line six times;
in verse 4 they sing their lines three times.

Abraham Maraire

251

45

O PRAISE THE NAME *From a Tumbuka Wedding song*

Doh is G

Leader

```
{ :m |m :— :m |m :— :r |d :— :s, |— :— :— |   :   :   |   :   :   }
{    O praise thename of |Je - sus,                                }
{                                    Chorus  O praise  the name of }
{ :   |   :   :   |   :   :   |   :   :   |   : :m |m :— :m |m :— :r}
{ :   |   :   :   |   :   :   |   :   :   |   : :d |d :— :d |d :— :s,}

{   :   :   |   :   :   |   :   :   |   : :s |s :— :s |s :— :s }
{                                          O praise  the name of }
{ Je - sus,    our King,                                         }
{ d :— :— |s, :— :l, |s, :— :— |— :— :   |   :   :   |   :   :  }
{ l, :— :— |m, :— :r, |d, :— :— |— :— :   |   :   :   |   :   :  }

{ l :s :— |   :   :   |   : :s |s :— :s |l :— :— |— :— :s }
{ Je-sus            Our King   our King,          O     }
{           Our King           our King,          Our   }
{   :   :   |   : :m |m :— :— |— :— :m |r :— :— |— :— :r }
{   :   :   |   : :d |d :— :— |— :— :d |l, :— :— |— :— :l,}

{ m :— :m |m :— :r |d :— :— |s, :— :   |   : :s |s :— :s }
{ praise thename of |Je -  sus        |     ourKing, our }
{ King,        our King,        Our King,          our   }
{ d :— :— |— :— :r |d :— :s, |— :— :m |m :— :— |— :— :m }
{ s, :— :— |— :— :l, |s, :— :— |— :— :d |d :— :— |— :— :d }

{ l :— :— |— :— :s |m :— :m |m :— :r |d :— :— |s, :— :m }
{ King,         O praise thename of Je - sus,    O      }
{ King,        our King,        our King,        O      }
{ r :— :— |— :— :r |d :— :— |— :— :r |d :— :s, |— :— :m }
{ l, :— :— |— :— :l, |s, :— :— |— :— :l, |s, :— :— |— :— :d}
```

```
 ⎧ m  :— :m |m  :— :r  | d  :— :— |s₁ :— :l₁ | s₁ :— :— |— :—  ‖
 ⎪ praise the name of |Je  -   sus,  our King.
 ⎨ praise the name of |Je  -   sus,  our King.
 ⎪ m  :— :m |m  :— :r  | d  :— :— |s₁ :— :l₁ | s₁ :— :— |— :—  ‖
 ⎩ d  :— :d |d  :— :s₁ | l₁ :— :— |m₁ :— :r₁ | d₁ :— :— |— :—  ‖
```

1 * O praise the name of Jesus
   *   *O praise the name of Jesus, our King*
  * O praise the name of Jesus
     Our King, our King, *our King*
  * O praise the name of Jesus
     Our King, our King,
     Our King, our King, *our King,*
  * O praise the name of Jesus
     Our King, our King,
  * O praise the name of Jesus, Our King.

In succeeding verses, substitute the lines marked*
   with the following:

2   He calls you all to hear Him
    He calls you all to hear Him, our King.

3   O turn your hearts unto Him
    O turn your hearts unto Him, our King.

4   For Christ our King is coming
    For Christ our King is coming, our King.

5   Then bring your offerings to Him
    Then bring your offerings to Him, our King.

6   Come with them all to Jesus
    Come with them all to Jesus, our King.

Ben Nhlane

Note: *This version of the words conforms more closely to the
music than that printed in the 'Words only' edition.*

46

WE PRAISE HIM   *Arranged by Nyakatsapa Vabyawi, Shona*
Doh is C   *[revised A.M.J.]*

Moderate and strong

Percussion

x	:	:		x	:	:		x	:	:		x	:x	:x	
d'	:d'		—	:m'	r'	:r'		m' .d'	:—	l	.l	:l		—	:l
O	Lamb		of	God	on		high,		O	we	praise		Him,

O Lamb of God on high, O we praise Him,

d' :d' |— :m' | r' :r' |m' .d' :— | m .m :m |— :m
d' :d' |— :m' | r' :r' |m' .d' :— | m' .m' :m' |— :m'
d' :d' |— :m' | r' :r' |m' .d' :— | l .l :l |— :l

Repeat

x : : |x : : |x : : |x :x :x ||
d :d |— :m |d :— |m :— | l .l :l |— :l
A - le - lu - ya,   O we praise Him!
s, :s, |— :t, | s, :— |t, :— | m .m :m |— :m
s :s |— :t | s :— |t :— | m' .m' :m' |— :m'
d :d |— :m | d :— |m : | l .l :l |— :l

x : : |x : : |x : : |x :x :x }

Leader   *Chorus*
d' :r' |d' :t' |l :s |f :f ||l .l :l |— :l }
1 Je - sus came on earth to save us,
2 We were bound by chains of fear,   O we praise Him,

: | : | : | : ||m .m :m |— :m
: | : | : | : ||m' .m' :m' |— :m'
: | : | : | : ||l .l :l |— :l

x : : |x : : |x : : |x :x :x }
d :d |— :m |d :— |m :— | l .l :l |— :l
A - le - lu - ya,   O we praise Him!
s, :s, |— :t, | s, :— |t, :— | m .m :m |— :m
s :s |— :t | s :— |t :— | m' .m' :m' |— :m'
d :d |— :m | d :— |m :— | l .l :l |— :l

Shona Hymn

×	:	:	×	:	:	×	:	:	×	:×	:×

Chorus

| : | | : | | : | | : | 1 | .1 | :1 | 1— | :1 |

Leader

	:			:		:	O we praise	Him,
d'	:r'	d'	:t	1	:s	f	:f	m	.m	:m	1—	:m
1 Life	and hope	He came	to give	us,	m'	.m'	:m'	1—	:m'
2 God's	great love	has set	us	free,	1	.1	:1	1—	:1

×	:	:	×	:	:	×	:	:	×	:×	:×
d	:d	1—	:m	d	:—	m	:—	1	.1	:1	1—	:1
A - le	-	lu - ya,	O we praise	Him!
s₁	:s₁		:t₁	s₁	:—	t₁	:—	m	.m	:m	1—	:m
s	:s		:t	s	:—	t	:—	m'	.m'	:m'	1—	:m'
d	:d	1—	:m	d	:—	m	:—	1	.1	:1	1—	:1

×	:	:	×	:	:	×	:	:	×	:×	:×
d'	:d'	1—	:m'	r'	:r'	m'.d'	:—	1	.1	:1	1—	:1
O Lamb	of	God on	high,	O we praise	Him,
d'	:d'	1—	:m'	r'	:r'	m'.d'	:—	m	.m	:m	1—	:m
d'	:d'	1—	:m'	r'	:r'	m'.d'	:—	m'	.m'	:m'	1—	:m'
d'	:d'	1—	:m'	r'	:r'	m'.d'	:—	1	.1	:1	1—	:1

×	:	:	×	:	:	×	:	:	×	:×	:×	×:	:
d	:d	1—	:m	d	:—	m	:—	1	.1	:1	1—	:1	:	:
A - le	-	lu - ya,	O we praise	Him!
s₁	:s₁	1—	:t₁	s₁	:—	t₁	:—	m	.m	:m	1—	:m	:	:
s	:s	1—	:t	s	:—	t	:—	m'	.m'	:m'	1—	:m'	:	:
d	:d	1—	:m	d	:—	m	:—	1	.1	:1	1—	:1	:	:

3 Why did God create us men? O, we praise Him!
Aleluya, O we praise Him!
He created us to praise Him, O we praise Him!
Aleluya, O we praise Him!

Shona Hymn

53

CREATOR AND FATHER

Doh is G

```
{ :d |d  :d :m |m  :r :d .r |m  :d :r  |t, :— :m |m  :m :s, |s  :f  )
{ :d |d  :d :s, |s, :s, :m,.s, |s, :s, :l, |s, :— :s, |s, :s, :d |d  :t, }
{ :m |m  :m :d |d  :t, :d .t, |d  :d :f  |r  :— :d |d  :d :m |m  :r  }
{ :d |d  :d :d |d  :t, :d .t, |d  :m, :f, |s, :— :d |d  :d :m |m  :r  )
```

```
{ :m .f |s  :m :f |r  :— :m |s  :f :r .m |f  :m :d |r  :r :f |m  :— ||
{ :d .t, |d  :s, :l, |s, :— :s, |d  :t, :s,.s, |t, :s, :m, |s, :s, :t, |d  :— ||
{ :d .r |m  :m :f |t, :— :d |m  :r :t,.d |r  :d :l, |t, :t, :r |d  :— ||
{ :d .r |m  :d :f, |s, :— :d |m  :r :t,.d |r  :d :l, |s, :s, :s, |d, :— ||
```

1 Creator and Father, Thou who rulest above,
Creator and Father, Thou who rulest above,
Come visit us Thy people in mercy and love.

2 Thou knowest in pathways of evil we stay,
Thou knowest in pathways of evil we stay,
O send Thy holy Spirit to teach us to-day.

3 O Spirit, enlighten our spirits within,
O Spirit, enlighten our spirits within,
And show us in Thy mercy wherein we do sin.

4 To Thee do we yield us, O show us Thy way,
To Thee do we yield us, O show us Thy way,
To Thee do we offer our own wills to-day.

5 O teach us to do what is good in Thy sight,
O teach us to do what is good in Thy sight,.
For all that Thou willest is perfect and right.

6 Our Father in heaven, O hear when we pray,
Our Father in heaven, O hear when we pray,
And grant us in Thy mercy Thy blessing to-day.

Jonathan Chirwa

60

Doh is B♭

Nsenga tune: Zambia

Leader | Irregular

S	:			:		:		:
	Heaven-ly	Fa	–	ther	Lord	of	all
A	:			:		:		:
T1	:d'	.r'	d'	:s	:l	.r'	d'	:—
T2	:			:		:		:
B	:			:		:		:

Chorus · Repeat

m	.m	:m	.m	m	.m	:r	d	:—
We	thy	child – ren	thank	and	praise	Thee	
t,	.t,	:t,	.t,	t,	.t,	:l,	s,	:—
m'	.m'	:m'	.m'	m'	.m'	:r'	d'	:—
t	.t	:t	.t	t	.t	:l	s	:—
m	.m	:m	.m	m	.m	:r	d	:—

r	.r	:r	.r	m	.r	:d	l,	:—
For	thy	good – ness	in	cre	a	–	tion
l,	.l,	:l,	.l,	t,	.l,	:s,	m,	:—
r'	.r'	:r'	.r'	m'	.r'	:d'	l	:—
l	.l	:l	.l	t	.l	:s	m	:—
r	.r	:r	.r	m	.r	:d	l,	:—

d	.d	:d	.d	:r	.d	:l,	s,	:—
And	the	grace	of	our	sal – va	–	tion
s,	.s,	:s,	.s,	:l,	.s,	:m,	r,	:—
d'	.d'	:d'	.d'	:r'	.d'	:l	s	:—
s	.s	:s	.s	:l	.s	:m	r	:—
d	.d	:d	.d	:r	.d	:l,	s,	:—

m	.r	:d	.r	:m	.m	:r	d	:—
Now	are	sung	in	ev -	ery	na -	tion,	
t,	.l,	:s,	.l,	:t,	.t,	:l,	s,	:—
m'	.r'	:d'	.r'	:m'	.m'	:r'	d'	:—
t	.l	:s	.l	:t	.t	:l	s	:—
m	.r	:d	.r	:m	.m	:r	d	:—

(The first two lines in each verse are repeated)

1   L: Heavenly Father, Lord of all

      C: *We Thy children thank and praise Thee;*
         For Thy goodness in creation
         And the grace of our salvation
         Now are sung in every nation.

2   L: Blessed Jesus, Son of God

      C: *We Thy children thank and praise Thee;*
         Once a Cross of pain Thou bearest,
         Now a Crown of Glory wearest,
         And Thy joy with us Thou sharest.

3   L: Holy Spirit, God of love

      C: *We Thy children thank and praise Thee,*
         By Thy grace and strong protection,
         Keep us true to Thy direction,
         Fill us with Divine affection.

4   L: Father, Son and Holy Ghost

      C: *We Thy children thank and praise Thee;*
         Till in heaven with saints surrounded
         We have known Thy joy unbounded,
         And Thy praise with gladness sounded.

Original in Cilala by A.M.Jones; altd.

61

John Mgandu, Tabora

Doh is G

{| l   :s | m   :r | m   .d   :—   d | l,   :— | l,   :s,   }

Fa - ther,   Fa - ther   all   of   us   praise   Thee   we

{| l,   .l,   :l,   .l, | l,   :l, | 1,   :— || r   .r   :—   .r   }

glo - ri - fy   Thy   Ho - ly   Name.   Cre - a   -   tor

Repeat

{| m   :d | l,   .l,   :l, | l,   :— | r   .r   :—   .r   }

Migh - ty,   Lord   of   all   power,   Cre - a   -   tor

{| m   :d | l,   .l,   :l, | l,   :s, | l,   .l,   :l,   .l, | l,   :l,   }

Migh - ty,   Lord of   all   power, We   glo - ri - fy   Thy Ho - ly

Repeat

{| l,   :— || m   :m | m   :r | m   .d   :—   .d   }

Name.   Fa - ther,   Fa - ther,   all   of   us

{| l,   :— | l,   :s, | l,   .l,   :l,   .l, | l,   :l, | 1,   :— ||

praise   Thee, We   glo - ri - fy   Thy Ho - ly   Name.

2 Jesus, Jesus, Thou art our Saviour, } *sing twice*
    We glorify thy Holy Name:
  Give us the grace to follow thy Way,⎫
  Give us the grace to follow thy Way ⎬ *sing twice*
    And glorify thy Holy Name.⎭
  Jesus, Jesus, Thou art our Saviour
    We glorify thy Holy Name.

3 Holy Spirit, strengthen our longing } *sing twice*
    To glorify thy Holy Name:
  Spirit of wisdom, Spirit of power ⎫
  Spirit of wisdom, Spirit of power ⎬ *sing twice*
    We glorify thy Holy Name.⎭
  Holy Spirit, strengthen our longing
    To glorify thy Holy Name.

4 Trinity of infinite glory } *sing twice*
    O blessed be thy Holy Name:
  One in Three Persons, Thee we adore ⎫
  One in Three Persons, Thee we adore ⎬ *sing twice*
    O blessed be thy Holy Name.⎭
  Trinity of infinite glory
    O blessed be thy Holy Name.

A. M. Jones

66

WE REMEMBER THEE

Doh is C

```
{|:d .d |s .s :m .r | d   :r  |— :d'.r'| m'  :r'.d' |l  :d' )
 |:d .d |s .s :m .r | d   :t, |— :s .s | s   :s .s  |f  :f   }
 |:d .d |s .s :m .r | d   :s  |— :d'.t | d'  :t .d' |d' :d'  }
 |:d .d |s .s :m .r | d   :s, |— :m .s | d   :s .m  |f  :l   )
```

```
{| s  :— |— :s .s | l  :s .m |r  :— .r | d  :— |— :— ||
 | m  :— |— :d .d | d  :d .d |t, :— .t,| d  :— |— :— ||
 | d' :— |— :m .m | f  :m .d |s  :— .f | m  :— |— :— ||
 | d' :— |— :m .m | f  :m .d |s, :— .s,| d  :— |— :— ||
```

1   We remember Thee, Lord Jesus,
Thou didst die for us on the tree:
Hear us now when we cry to Thee.

2   We remember Thee, Lord Jesus,
For Thy life's blood was shed in pain,
And Thy body for us was slain

3   We remember Thee, Lord Jesus,
When we taste of the bread and wine;
In this sacrament make us Thine.

Thomas Ngoma

75

WHEN I CALLED   *Wedding Song, Malaŵi*

Doh is G
When three parts sing, the main tune is in the middle part.
Leader

```
 ⎧ d  :— :d |d :— :r │ d  :— :— |d :— :— ‖ m  :— :m |m :— :m ⎫
 ⎪ When  I called  to│ Je  -   sus     ‖ When  I called  to ⎪
 ⎨    :  : |  :  :   │    :  : |  :  :  ‖ l  :— :l |l :— :l  ⎬
 ⎩ m₁ :— :m₁|m₁:— :r₁│ d₁ :— :— |d₁:— :— ‖ d  :— :d |d :— :d ⎭
```

```
                                        ┌ 1             D.C.┐
 ⎧ m  :— :— |m :— :r │ d  :— :s |m :— :r │ d  :— :— |— :— :— ‖
 ⎪ Je  -   sus He   │ ans-wered me  in │ love               ‖
 ⎨ l  :— :— |l :— :s │ m  :— :r |d :— :r │ d  :— :— |— :— :— ‖
 ⎩ d  :— :— |d :— :s₁│ s₁ :— :s₁|s₁:— :s₁│ d₁ :— :— |— :— :— ‖
```

```
 ┌ 2   Chorus
         He is    my Sav   -    -    iour,  He is    my
 ⎧ d  :— :s |m :— :r │ d  :— :— |— :— :— │ r  :— :s |m :— :r ⎫
 ⎪ love              │ Sav  -    -    iour,                  ⎪
 ⎨ d  :— :— |  :  :  │ m  :— :— |— :— :— │ r  :— :— |  :  :  ⎬
 ⎩ d₁ :— :— |  :  :  │ d  :— :— |l₁:— :— │ s₁ :— :— |  :  :  ⎭
```

```
   Sav      -       iour
 ⎧ d  :— :— |— :— :— │ r  :— :— |— :— :d │ d  :— :s |m :— :r ⎫
 ⎪ Sav      -       iour,          He   │ ans-wered me  in  ⎪
 ⎨ m  :— :— |— :— :— │ r  :— :— |— :— :m │ m  :— :r |d :— :r ⎬
 ⎩ d  :— :— |l₁:— :— │ s₁ :— :— |— :— :s₁│ s₁ :— :s₁|s₁:— :s₁⎭
```

He is   my Sav   -   iour, He is   my Sav   -

```
{ | d :—:s |m :—:r | d :—:— |—:—:— | r :—:s |m :—:r | d :—:— |—:—:— \
  | love            | Sav    -         | iour,           | Sav    -        |
  | d :—:— | :  :   | m :—:— |—:—:— | r :—:— | :  :   | m :—:— |—:—:— |
  | d, :—:— | :  :  | d :—:— ||1, :—:— | s, :—:— | :  :  | d :—:— ||1, :—:— /
```

iour

```
{ | r :— :— |— :— :d | d :— :s |m :— :r | d :— :— |— :— :— \
  | iour            | He | ans - wered me in | love .          ||
  | r :— :— |— :— :m | m :— :r |d :— :r | d :— :— |— :— :— |
  | s, :— :— |— :— :s, | s, :— :s, |s, :— :s, | d, :— :— |— :— :— ||
```

2 L: **When I prayed for mercy**
   C: **When I prayed for mercy He answered
      me in love.**

     (whole verse to be repeated)
     Chorus

3 L: **When I cried unto Him**
   C: **When I cried unto Him He answered .
      me in love.**

     (whole verse to be repeated)
     Chorus

4 L: **When I came to Jesus**
   C: **When I came to Jesus He answered
      me in love.**

     (whole verse to be repeated)
     Chorus

Mawelera Tembo

123

GOD BLESS AFRICA

Doh is G

d	.d	:d	.r	|m	:m	r	:r	|d	:—
Bless	O	Lord	our	land	of	A	-	fri -	ca
s,	.s,	:s,	.s,	|d	:d	t,	:t,	|s,	:—
m	.m	:m	.f	|s	:s	f	:f	|m	:—
d	.d	:d	.d	|d	:d	s,	:s,	|d,	:—

m	.m	:m	.m	|f	:f	m	:m	|r	:—
Lift	its	name	and	make	its	peo -	ple	free	
d	.d	:d	.d	|l,	:t,	d	:d	|t,	:—
s	.s	:s	.s	|f	:s	s	:s	|s	:f
d	.d	:d	.d	|r	:r	d	:d	|s,	:—

d	.d	:d	.r	|m	:m	r	:f	|m	:—
Take	the	gifts	we	o -	ffer	un -	to	Thee,	
l,	.l,	:l,	.t,	|d	:d	l,	:t,	|d	:—
m	.m	:m	.s	|s	:s	f	:s	|s	:—
l,	.l,	:l,	.s,	|d	:d	r	:r	|m	:d

r	:—	|d	:—	t, .d	:r	|d	:—	r	:—	|d	:—
Hear		us		faith -	ful	sons,		hear		us	
l,	:—	|s,	:—	s,	:t,	|s,	:—	l,	:—	|s,	:—
f	:—	|m	:—	r .m	:f	|m	:—	f	:—	|m	:—
f,	:—	|s,	:—	s,	:s,	|d	:—	f	:—	|s,	:—

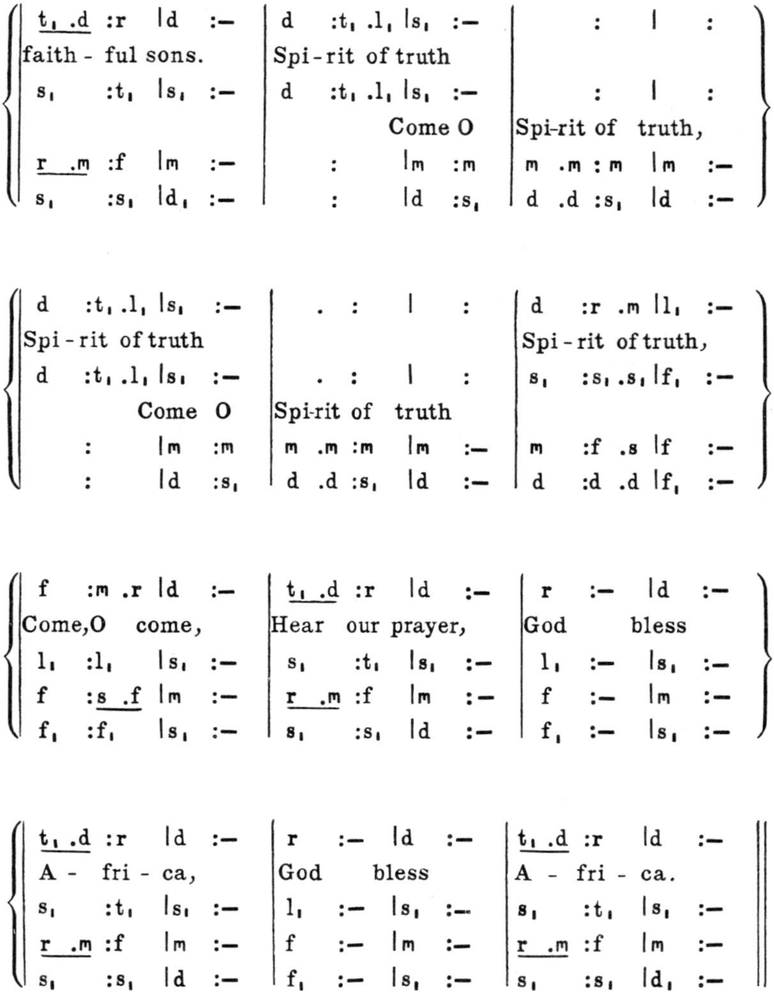
faith - ful sons.
Spi - rit of truth
Come O
Spi-rit of truth,
Spi - rit of truth
Spi - rit of truth,
Come O
Spi-rit of truth
Come, O come,
Hear our prayer,
God bless
A - fri - ca,
God bless
A - fri - ca.

126

LORD HAVE MERCY
Doh is F

In free rhythm

Missa Mikaeli Mtakatifu
David Powell (adapted)

Sing 3 times

Leader   Chorus

{| s :- |m :s |f :m |r :- ‖ f :r |m :d .d |r :t, |d :- ‖

Lord,_____ have mer-cy u - pon us,

Sing 3 times

Leader   Chorus

{| s :- |l :s :m |d :- ‖ r |r :m |d :d |r :d |s, :- ‖

Christ,_____ have mer - cy u - pon us,

Sing 3 times

Leader   Chorus

{| s :- |m :s |f :m |r :- ‖ f :r |m :d .d |r :t, |d :- ‖

Lord,_____ have mer-cy u - pon us.

127

HOLY, HOLY, HOLY Irregular   *Victor Mwachumo Chunga*

Doh is G

Leader   *Chorus*

```
{|   : |   :  |1 :-|-:- |s :-:-|m  :-:-|- :-||s :-|:-  )
 |       |    |Ho - |ly, |      |       |     ||Ho -      }
 {|   : |   :  |  : |  : |  :  :|  :   :|   :  ||s₁ :-|:- )
 {|   : |   :  |  : |  : |  :  :|  :   :|   :  ||r :-|:-  }
 {|   : |   :  |  : |  : |  :  :|  :   :|   :  ||m₁:-|:-  )
```

```
{|m :-:-|r :-:-|- :-|m :-|-:- |r :-:-|d :-:-|- :-:- )
 |ly,   |      |    |Ho - |ly, |      |      |           }
 {|m₁:- :-|s₁:-:-|- :-|l₁:-|-:-|s₁:-:-|m₁:-:-|- :-:- }
 {|d :-:-|l₁:-:-|- :-|d :-|-:- |l₁:-:-|s₁:-:-|- :-:-  }
 {|r₁:-:-|s₁:-:-|- :-|s₁:-|-:- |s₁:-:-|d₁:-:-|- :-:-  )
```

```
{|r :-:m|s :-:-|- :-|l :-|-:- |s :-:-|m :-:-|r :-|r :- )
 |Lord |God   |    |of  |    |Hosts,|      |Hea - ven    }
 {|s₁:-:m₁|s₁:-:-|- :-|l₁:-|-:-|s₁:-:-|l₁:-:-|s₁:-|s₁:- }
 {|r :-:d|r :-:-|- :-|m :-|-:- |r :-:-|d :-:-|r :-|r :-  }
 {|s₁:-:m₁|s₁:-:-|- :-|l₁:-|-:-|s₁:-:-|d₁:-:-|s₁:-|s₁:-  )
```

```
{|m :-|s :-:-|- :-|d :-|r :-|m :-|-:- |- :-|-:- |r :-|m :- )
 |and earth |    |are |    |full|     |    |    |of  thy     }
 {|m₁:-|s₁:-:-|- :-|m₁:-|r₁:-|s₁:-|-:-|- :-|-:- |s₁:-|s₁:- }
 {|d :-|r :-:-|- :-|d :-|l₁:-|s₁:-|-:-|- :-|-:- |r :-|r :-  }
 {|m₁:-|s₁:-:-|- :-|l₁:-|s₁:-|d₁:-|-:-|- :-|-:- |s₁:-|s₁:-  )
```

```
{|s :-:-|m :-:-|r :-:-|d :-|-:-|- :-|-:- |s :-|s :- )
 |glo   |  -   |  -   |ry  |    |    |    |Ho - sa -     }
 {|s₁:-:-|l₁:-:-|s₁:-:-|m₁:-|-:-|- :-|-:-|s₁:-|s₁:- }
 {|r :-:-|d :-:-|l₁:-:-|d :-|-:-|- :-|-:- |r :-|r :-  }
 {|s₁:-:-|d₁:-:-|s₁:-:-|d₁:-|-:-|- :-|-:- |m₁:-|m₁:-  )
```

```
{|m :-:-|r :-:-|- :-|d :-|m :-|r :-:-|d :-:-|- :-:-|- :-:- )
 |na,   |      |    |in  |the |high - est.|       |          }
 {|m₁:-:-|s₁:-:-|- :-|l₁:-|l₁:-|s₁:-:-|m₁:-:-|- :-:-|- :-:- }
 {|d :-:-|l :-:-|- :-|d :-|d :-|l₁:-:-|s₁:-:-|- :-:-|- :-:-  }
 {|r₁:-:-|s₁:-:-|- :-|s₁:-|s₁:-|s₁:-:-|d₁:-:-|- :-:-|- :-:-  )
```

128

LAMB OF GOD   *Miles Manyawu*

Doh is F

Slowly

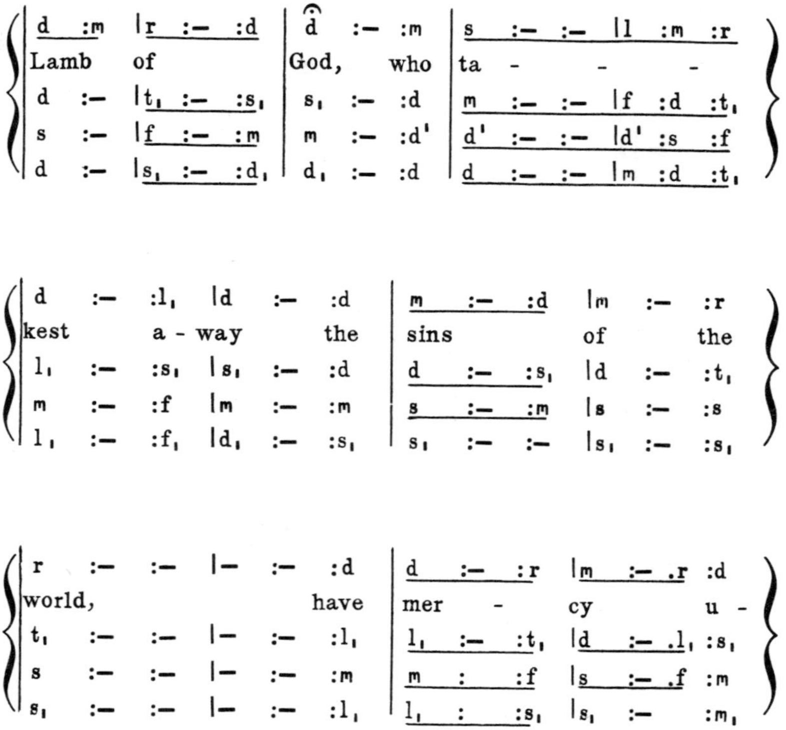

r :— :—	d :— :—	‖ d :m	r :— :d
pon	us;	Lamb	of
t₁ :— :l₁	s₁ :— :—	d :—	t₁ :— :s₁
f :— :—	m :— :—	s :—	f :— :m
s₁ :— :—	d₁ :— :—	d :—	s₁ :— :d₁

d͡ :— :m	s :— :—	l :m :r	d :— :l₁	d :— :d
God, who	ta —	—	kest a - way	the
s₁ :— :d	m :— :—	f :d :t₁	l₁ :— :s₁	s₁ :— :d
m :— :d'	d' :— :—	d' :s :f	m :— :f	m :— :m
d₁ :— :d	d :— :—	m :d :t₁	l₁ :— :f₁	d₁ :— :s₁

m :— :d	m :— :r	r :— :—	— :— :—
sins	of	the world,	
d :— :s₁	d :— :t₁	t₁ :— :—	— :— :—
s :— :m	s :— :s	s :— :—	— :— :—
s₁ :— :—	s₁ :— :s₁	s₁ :— :—	— :— :—

d :— :r	m :— .r :d	r :— :—	d :— :—
grant	us	peace.	
l₁ :— :t₁	d :— .l₁ :s₁	t₁ :— :l₁	s₁ :— :—
m :— :f	s :— .f :m	f :— :—	m :— :—
l₁ :— :s₁	s₁ :— :m₁	s₁ :— :—	d₁ :— :—

129

LAUDAMUS   *from the Zulu Church*

Doh is C   *Irregular*

{| d' :l :− .s | s :− || d' :d' | l :−.s | s :− ||

Save us   dear Lord,   bless your he - ri - tage;

{| s :s | l :−.s | s :− || r :r ,r ,m :r :−.d :d :− ||

Go-vern us   with love,   and lift us up for   e -ver.

{| d :m :f | s :− :s | s :s :s | l :− | s :− ||

We mag-ni - fy   you day by day dear   Lord

{| d :m | f :s :− :s ,s ,s | l :− | s :− ||

Now and   e - ver   we wor-ship your   name.

{| s :s ,s ,s | l :− | s :− || d' | d' :− | d' :d' }

Pro-mise to keep us,   Lord,   this   day   with-out

{| l :l | s :s | f :m | r :r | m :− || f }

sin. Have mer - cy   u -   pon us Lord.   Have

*Each phrase may sung twice, first by the leader and then by the
congregation.*

272

{|m :r :– |d :– ||d :m :f |s :– |l :– |s :– ||
mer-cy   Lord.   As we have trust   in   you,

{|s :l |s :– ||d' :d' |l :– |s :l |f :m }
on - ly you,   Let not your   ser-vants be con -

{|r :– |m :– ||s :f :m |r :d |r :r |d :– ||
foun - ded.   E - ver - more we wor-ship you,

{|d' :d' |d' .d' :d' :d' |l :– |s :– ||
E - ver more we mag - ni - fy   you;

{|d' :d'.d'|d' :d' |l :– |s :– ||s :s .s |s :s .s }
And e-ver-more we trust you;   Lord keep us not with-out

{|l :s |f :m |r :– |d :– ||d' .d' :d' :d' }
sin, Have mer - cy on   us.   Save your peo - ple

{|l :– |s :– |d'.d' :d' :d' |l :l |s :– ||s |f :m|r :– |d :– ||
O   Lord, E-ver bless your he-ri-tage. A - - men.

Engraved and Printed by Lowe and Brydone (Printers) Limited, London

DAILY WORSHIP

INTRODUCTION

The main elements of school worship are: hymns, Bible reading and prayers. The prayers themselves can be divided into:

Praise and Thanksgiving

Petition (prayers for ourselves)

Intercession (prayers for others).
The prayers in this book have been divided into these three subjects.

Many schools are used to the familiar pattern of: hymn—Bible reading—prayers. It is good to vary this as far as possible. It will be noted that very often the hymn chosen is itself a prayer; it may be of praise, thanksgiving, or petition. When this is the case, this aspect of prayer need not be included in the prayers chosen; they can be from the other two sections.

In the section on Intercession, there are five subsections; this will enable a school to work out a system of praying for a different need on each of the five days of the week.

Some of the prayers are best read by the leader and followed silently by the children. Others may be read by leader and children speaking together. Others allow for responses to be spoken by the children. These responses are shown by being printed in italics. It is suggested that children should take an active part in at least one of the prayers each morning.

SUGGESTED ORDERS FOR
MORNING PRAYERS

1 Prayer of Praise and Thanksgiving
Hymn from "Our Life as Christians" section
Reading
Prayer of Intercession
The Lord's Prayer.

2 Hymn of Praise and Thanksgiving
Reading
Prayer of Petition
Prayer of Intercession
Benediction.

3 Reading: Psalm of Praise
Hymn
Prayer of Petition
Prayer of Intercession
Benediction.

SUGGESTIONS FOR REGULAR
READINGS FROM THE BIBLE

Psalms: 1, 8, 23, 24, 27, 33, 46, 63, 84, 90, 95, 103, 139, 148.
Matthew: 5: 38–48; 6: 25–33; 7: 21–27; 25: 31–46.
Mark: 1: 9–20; 4: 1–9; 4: 26–34; 10: 17–22.
Luke: 4: 1–13; 7: 1–10; 10: 25–37; 11: 1–13; 15: 1–24.
John: 1: 1–14; 10: 11–18; 14: 1–7; 15: 1–17; 20: 1–18.
Romans 8: 28–39; 1 Corinthians 13: 1–13; Galatians 5: 16–25;
Ephesians 3: 14–21; 6: 10–18; I John 4: 17–21; Revelation 7:
9–17.

THE OLD TESTAMENT COMMANDMENTS

GOD spoke these words, and said:
I am the Lord your God; you shall have no other gods
before me.
Lord, have mercy upon us, and incline our hearts to keep this law.

You shall not make yourself a graven image, or any likeness of
anything that is in heaven above, or that in is the earth
beneath, or that is in the water under the earth; you shall
not bow down to them or serve them.
Lord have mercy upon us, and incline our hearts to keep this law.

You shall not take the name of the Lord your God in vain.
Lord, have mercy upon us, and incline our hearts to keep this law.

Remember the sabbath day, to keep it holy.
Lord, have mercy upon us, and incline our hearts to keep this law.

Honour your father and your mother.
Lord, have mercy upon us, and incline our hearts to keep this law.

You shall not kill.
Lord, have mercy upon us, and incline our hearts to keep this law.

You shall not commit adultery.
Lord, have mercy upon us, and incline our hearts to keep this law.

You shall not steal.
Lord, have mercy upon us, and incline our hearts to keep this law.

You shall not bear false witness against your neighbour.
Lord, have mercy upon us, and incline our hearts to keep this law.

You shall not covet.
Lord, have mercy upon us and write these laws in our hearts.

The Commandments of The Lord Jesus

JESUS said: The first of all the commandments is:
You shall love the Lord your God with all your heart,
and with all your soul, and with all your mind. This is the
great and first commandment.
Lord, have mercy upon us, and incline our hearts to keep this law.

The second is this: You shall love your neighbour as yourself.
Lord, have mercy upon us, and incline our hearts to keep this law.

This is my commandment, that you love one another as I have
loved you.
Lord, have mercy upon us, and incline our hearts to keep this law.

Jesus said: He who has my commandments and keeps them,
he it is who loves me; and he who loves me will be loved by
my Father, and I will love him and manifest myself to him.
Lord, have mercy upon us, and write these laws in our hearts.

THE PERFECT LIFE

Blessed are the poor in spirit:
For theirs is the kingdom of heaven.

Blessed are those who mourn:
For they shall be comforted.

Blessed are the meek:
For they shall inherit the earth.

Bleesed are those who hunger and thirst for righteousness:
For they shall be satisfied.

Blessed are the merciful:
For they shall obtain mercy.

Blessed are the pure in heart:
For they shall see God.

Blessed are the peacemakers:
For they shall be called sons of God.

Blessed are those who are persecuted for righteousness' sake:
For theirs is the kingdom of heaven.

THE APOSTLES' CREED

I BELIEVE in God the Father Almighty, maker of heaven
and earth: and in Jesus Christ His only Son our Lord;
who was conceived by the Holy Ghost, born of the virgin
Mary, suffered under Pontius Pilate, was crucified, dead and
buried; He descended into hell, the third day He rose again
from the dead, He ascended into heaven, and sits on the right
hand of God the Father Almighty; from thence He shall come
to judge the quick and the dead.

I believe in the Holy Ghost, the holy Catholic Church, the
communion of saints, the forgiveness of sins, the resurrection
of the body, and the life everlasting. *Amen.*

278

A Christian's Belief

I BELIEVE in God, the Maker of all things and our Heavenly Father, whose power and wisdom are seen in the heavens above, in the world around, and in the life that is in us and in all living things.

I believe in Jesus Christ, our Lord, Leader, Saviour and Friend; who was once a baby in Bethlehem; who, as a boy in Nazareth, grew in wisdom and in stature; who loved men and women and children; who healed those that were ill; who taught men about our Father, and showed them what He is like; whose love is a pattern for our love; who was tempted as we are; who died on the Cross to save us from our sins and bring us to love Him; who rose from the dead and is with us always.

I believe in the Holy Spirit, who dwells in us all, who teaches us what is right and true and beautiful, and gives us strength to do God's will. And I believe in the fellowship of all who love and follow Jesus, which is His Church.

I believe that we are in the hand of God our Father, who forgives our sins, and has prepared a home in heaven for all who love Him.

PRAYERS

PRAISE AND THANKSGIVING

1 YOU are my God, and I will praise you:
  You are my God, and I will thank you.
Bless the Lord, O my soul,
And all that is within me, bless his holy name.
Holy, holy, holy, Lord God almighty,
Heaven and earth are full of your glory;
Glory be to you, O Lord most high. *Amen.*

2 GOD be merciful unto us, and bless us, and show us
  the light of your glory.
That your way may be known upon earth,
  your saving health among all nations.
Let the people praise you, O God;
Yes, let all the people praise you.
Then shall the earth rejoice and be glad,
And God, even our own God, shall give us his
  blessing. *Amen.*

3 PRAISE be to you, O God the father,
  Who has made of one blood all nations on the
 earth.
Praise be to you, O God the son,
  Who has saved all men from the fear of evil.
Praise be to you, O God the Holy Spirit,
  Who has given light and life to men,
  And fills us all with hope.
Praise and glory be to you, Father, Son, and Holy
  Spirit. *Amen.*

4 GLORY be to God on high,
  And on earth peace, goodwill towards men.
We praise you, we bless you,
We worship you, we give glory to you,
We give thanks to you for your great glory,
  O Lord God, heavenly king,
  God the Father almighty. *Amen.*

5 ALMIGHTY God, Father of all mercies, we your unworthy servants, do give you most humble and hearty
thanks for all your goodness and loving-kindness to us, and
to all mankind. We bless you for our creation, preservation,
and all the blessings of this life; but above all, for your
inestimable love in the redemption of the world by our Lord
Jesus Christ; for the means of grace and for the hope of
glory, through Jesus Christ, our Lord. *Amen.*

6 YOU are worthy, O Lord, to receive power,

> And riches,
> And wisdom,
> And strength,
> And honour,
> And glory,
> And blessing.

We thank you for the light of the everlasting gospel, sent
forth to every nation, language, race, and family.
We thank you for your Church, which has passed on the
truth through every generation, and which will never be
defeated.
All glory be to you, O Lord. *Amen.*

7 YOU are the great God, he who is in heaven.
You are the creator of life, who has made the heavens
above.
You are the hunter who hunts for souls.
You are the leader who goes before us.
You are the great mantle which covers us.
You are he whose hands are with wounds.
You are he whose feet are with wounds.
You are he whose blood was given for us.
Thanks be unto you, O God. *Amen.*

8 THANKS be to you, my Lord Jesus Christ,
For all the pains and insults you have suffered for me.

O most merciful Redeemer, Friend and Brother,
May I know you more clearly,
May I love you more dearly,
May I follow you more nearly. *Amen.*

281

9 OUR Heavenly Father,
    We thank you for the world and all your good gifts,
For the sky above us, and the earth beneath our feet,
For our homes and our friends,
For your power and love which guard us,
And, most of all,
For the life and example of Jesus Christ your Son, our
    Lord. *Amen.*

Petition for Ourselves

10 O GOD our heavenly Father,
    Forgive us for all our faults remembered and
    forgotten;
For the things we ought to have done and have not done,
For the things we have done which have brought sorrow to
    ourselves or others.
And as we pray that we may be forgiven,
Help us to forgive those who have done wrong to us,
    Through Jesus Christ our Lord. *Amen.*

11 ALMIGHTY and most merciful Father, we have erred
and strayed from your ways like lost sheep. We have
followed too much the devices and desires of our own
hearts. We have offended against your holy law. We have
left undone those things which we ought to have done and
we have done those things which we ought not to have
done, and there is no health in us. O Lord, have mercy
upon us miserable offenders. Spare those who are penitent,
according to your promises declared to men in Christ
Jesus, our Lord: and grant, most merciful Father, for his
sake, that we may hereafter live a godly, righteous and
sober life, to the glory of your holy name. *Amen.*

12 O GOD the Holy Spirit,
    Come to us, and come amongst us.
Come as the wind and make us clean;
Come as the fire and burn up our sin;
Come as the dew, and refresh us.
Come and convince us, so that we may willingly give our
    hearts and lives to serve you.
    We ask this for Jesus Christ's sake. *Amen.*

13 L ORD, we believe in you:
　　　Help us when our faith is weak.
　We love you,
　　　but not with the perfect hearts we wish for.
　We long for you,
　　　but not with our whole minds.
　Accept our faith,
　　　　our love,
　　　　our longing to know and serve you,
　　　　our trust in your power to keep us.
　Set fire to all that is cold in us,
　Supply all that is missing in our lives,
　　　Through Jesus Christ our Lord. *Amen.*

14 O ALMIGHTY God, who has gathered us together as
　　　members of one family in our school, grant that we
　may realize our responsibility to one another.
　May truth, honour, and kindness grow among us.
　May your blessing rest upon our work.
　May your name be hallowed in our midst, and your peace
　　　guard our hearts.
　　　Through Jesus Christ our Lord. *Amen.*

15 G RANT us, Lord, to worship you in spirit and in truth;
　　　To submit all our nature to you, so that
　　　our conscience may be made active by your holiness;
　　　our mind fed by your truth;
　　　our imagination made pure by your beauty.
　Help us to open our hearts to your love, and to surrender
　　　our wills to your purpose.
　So may we lift up our hearts to you in love,
　　　Through Jesus Christ our Lord. *Amen.*

16 A LMIGHTY God, to whom all thoughts are open, all
　　　desires known, and from whom no secrets are
　hidden; cleanse the thoughts of our hearts by the inspira-
　tion of your Holy Spirit, that we may perfectly love you,
　and worthily praise your holy name. Through Jesus Christ
　our Lord. *Amen.*

17 O GOD of truth, and light, and love,
We bring our worship to you.
Help us to learn to hate everything that you hate, and to love everything that you love, so that we may be your true children, to-day and always. *Amen.*

18 O GOD, to whom we always look, give light to our hearts, as the sun throws light upon the dark bushes around us.
May we always reflect your brightness, so that those who have not known you may see you in us.
In the name of the great light, Jesus Christ, we ask this.
Amen.

19 TEACH us, good Lord, to serve you as you deserve, to give and not to count the cost, to fight and not to heed the wounds, to toil and not to seek for rest, to labour and not to ask for any reward, except that of knowing that we do your will. Through Jesus Christ our Lord. *Amen.*

20 O LORD Jesus Christ, be with us to-day:
In the things we do,
In the words we speak,
In the thoughts we think,
In the way we work,
In the way we treat other people.
So may your kingdom come, and your will be done,
On earth as it is in heaven. *Amen.*

21 MAY the love of the lord Jesus draw us to himself.
May the power of the Lord Jesus strengthen us in his service;
May the joy of the Lord Jesus fill our souls. *Amen.*

22 COME, Lord! Come with me.
See with my eyes;
Hear with my ears;
Think with my mind
Love with my heart;
Work with my hands.

Take my will and make it yours;
Take my understanding and make it clear;
Take my love and direct it to yourself;
Take me, to go where you want,
    to do what you want, in your way. *Amen.*

23 LORD, come to us to cleanse us,
    Lord, come to us to heal us,
Lord, come to us to strengthen us;
And grant that, having received you,
We may never be separated from you by our sins, but be
    loyal to you for ever. *Amen.*

INTERCESSION FOR OTHERS
Our Homes and Our Neighbours

24 O GOD of all mercy, we remember in our prayers: our
    fathers and mothers; all our relations and friends; all
for whom we have a duty to pray; and all who have helped
us in the past.

Fill all their minds, we pray, with the knowledge and
power of your truth; and knit all hearts more closely to you
and each other.

Arise, O God, and show yourself to be
    the helper of the helpless;
    the light of the blind;
    the strength of the weak;
    the deliverer of the captive;
    the comforter of the sad;
    and the Saviour of all who put their trust in you.
        Through Jesus Christ our Lord. *Amen.*

25 O HEAVENLY Father, who has given us the joy of earthly
    family and friends, look in love upon our homes.

Protect our families from all harm;
Keep them from all fear;
Help them to remain faithful to all the truths that they have
    learnt;
Let no shadow come between them and us to divide our
    hearts.
Through Jesus Christ our Lord. *Amen.*

Our Country and Its Leaders

26 LET us pray for the . . . (President) and all members of the Government, that in all things thay may make decisions that are good for the whole country, and in accordance with the will of God.

Lord, hear our prayer.
And let our cry come unto you.

Let us pray for all Civil Servants, in the different ministries of the Government, that they may look upon their work as a service to others, and also for the glory of God.

Lord, hear our prayer.
And let our cry come unto you.

Let us pray for the representatives of our country overseas, and for all our countrymen who have travelled abroad, that they may find Christ wherever they are, and be faithful to him.

Lord, hear our prayer.
And let our cry come unto you. Amen.

27 ALMIGHTY and eternal God, Father of all men, into your hands we commend our land of . . .

Draw into closer unity all her peoples.

Send out your light and your truth so that they may lead us into ways of peace.

Deliver us from the pride that does not fear God.

Save us from the selfishness that does not think of the needs of other men.

Grant that our nation may be an instrument for good to all the nations of the world.

Strengthen us, we pray, that we may follow the will of Christ, and so continue to serve you to the end of time.

Through Jesus Christ our Lord. *Amen.*

28 ALMIGHTY God, in whose hands lies the destiny of nations, we pray that you will give to our . . . (President), and to all our leaders, vision and integrity: that our country may be a land where justice is denied to none, and opportunity is given to all.

Strengthen the efforts of the Government to help the poor, the uneducated, and the unemployed.

Direct the hearts of all who bear authority, and protect them from the pride of power and unworthy ambition, that they may seek first your kingdom and its righteousness, and find them in your son Jesus Christ, our Lord. *Amen.*

29 O GOD, the Father of all the people of the earth:
Look with favour on us, and hear the prayer we make for our country.
Bless all the people of our land.
Deliver us from all evil.
Heal our misunderstandings, and teach us to love one another.
Give wisdom to our rulers, and a spirit of obedience and loyalty to all our people.
We ask your Fatherly guidance, especially for our young men and women, upon whom the future depends.
Guide the work of our hands and the decisions of our leaders,
So that our country may deserve an honoured place among the nations. *Amen.*

30 O LORD God, who has decided that all men whatever their race or colour, are equal before you; break down the hatred between men, especially hatred due to national differences.

We ask you to help those in whose hands are the various governments of the world. Reconcile them to one another, so that each may respect the rights of the other.

We ask all this in the name of our Saviour, Jesus Christ.
Amen.

The World and Its Needs

31 LET us pray for all who are ill, and especially for any suffering from a long illness.
For the blind, the deaf, and the dumb, and for those suffering from leprosy,
Hear us, Lord, we pray.

For those suffering from painful diseases, and those who know that they will never get better.
Hear us, Lord, we pray.

For those who are worried, and whose worry is affecting· their work and their health.
Hear us, Lord, we pray.

For those who are suffering because of the sins of others, or because of their own sins,
Hear us, Lord, we pray.

For those who have not learned that you can help them when they suffer,
Hear our prayers, O Lord.   Amen.

32 LET us pray for all who are poor.
   Lord, hear our prayer:
   And let our cry come unto you.

Let us pray for those who need food and better homes.
   Lord, hear our prayer:
   And let our cry come unto you.

Let us pray for those who need health and strength.
   Lord, hear our prayer:
   And let our cry come unto you.

Let us pray for those who have no purpose in their lives.
   Lord, hear our prayer:
   And let our cry come unto you.

Let us pray for those who need work and cannot find it.
   Lord, hear our prayer:
   And let our cry come unto you.

Let us pray for all who are trying to help other people.
   Lord, hear our prayer:
   And let our cry come unto you.

Let us pray that God may open our eyes to see what can we
do to help those in need, and give us power to do it.
Lord, hear our prayer:
And let our cry come unto you.   Amen.

33 O GOD our Father in heaven, we pray for all nations, that
you will give them unity and peace.
Please hear us, Lord.

We ask that all nations may learn the meaning of our
Saviour's teaching, and may desire to help others before they
look for help; the that strong may help the weak; and that all
may serve the common good.
Please hear us, Lord.

We ask that the United Nations, by wise leadership and
the support of every nation, may succeed in establishing the
rule of goodwill, and may lead men to freedom and peace.
Please hear us, Lord.

We ask that our own people may learn to seek first your
righteousness and your kingdom.
Please hear us, Lord.

We pray that you will bless all who guide our policies and
make our laws; all who lead public opinion; all citizens of
this land; that the mind of the people may be wise, its heart
sound, and its will righteous.
Please hear our prayers, O Lord.   Amen.

34 O GOD, who in the person of your Son was quick to
deliver those in suffering, we pray for those who are
passing through hard times.

For those who have lost their health, and are unable to
take their place in the life that others lead; especially
those crippled, or blind, or those with leprosy.

For those who have no work, and for those who are
afraid of losing their work.

For those who are without food: especially children,
anxious mothers, the old and the sick.

For any among us now who are in special need of your strength, healing, and peace.

We commend to your fatherly goodness all those who are in any way distressed in mind, body or spirit; that it may please you to comfort them according to their different needs, giving them patience under their sufferings, and a happy release from all their troubles. This we ask for Jesus Christ's sake. *Amen.*

35 LORD Jesus Christ, you are the Lord of peace:
    make us instruments of your peace.
Where there is hatred, may we bring love;
Where there is injury, may we bring pardon;
Where there is division, may we bring unity;
Where there is doubt, may we bring faith;
Where there is despair, may we bring hope;
Where there is darkness, may we bring light;
Where there is sadness, may we bring joy;
    For your mercy and your truth's sake. *Amen.*

36 O GOD, we pray for all those who will be sitting for examinations in these coming days. May they be calm and good tempered, have a sound judgment in all things, and be free from stress in the face of unusual conditions; and grant that their efforts may meet with success. *Amen.*

Those Who Help Other People

37 LET us pray for all doctors, nurses, and others who care for the sick; that they may do their work faithfully and lovingly.
    Lord, hear our prayer:
    And let our cry come unto you.

Let us pray for all who are trying to prevent suffering by improving diet, by better hygiene, or in other ways.
    Lord, hear our prayer:
    And let our cry come unto you.

Let us pray that God will show us what we can do to help others, and strengthen us to do it.
    Lord, hear our prayer:
    And let our cry come unto you. Amen.

38 LET us pray for the Minister of Education, and all those who advise him, that they may so plan as to enable all children in this country to attend school.
Hear us, Lord, we pray.

Let us pray for all who carry out the day-to-day work of the schools: for Education Secretaries and Managers, that they may seek God's will in the work they do.
Hear us, Lord, we pray.

Let us pray for all teachers, that they may respect and love the children in their classes, and seek to satisfy God in their work.
Hear us, Lord, we pray.

Let us pray for all who have helped us in our education: for the Government that has paid for our schools; for relatives who have paid our fees; for teachers who have given their best to teach us.
Hear our prayer, O Lord.   Amen.

39 O LORD Jesus Christ, the great healer of body and of soul: bless all doctors, nurses, and orderlies, whom you have called to care for the sick and the suffering.

Give them skill and power.
Bless the remedies they use.
Help them always to remember that when they care for others thay are caring for you.
Give them grace to be tender and patient in all their work.
May their hearts be filled with sympathy and love.
May they exercise their skill for the wellbeing of mankind.
May they not only heal, but also help those who are distressed and afraid.   *Amen.*

The Church

40 LET us pray for the Church, that it may be courageous to bear witness to its Lord and to do his will.
Lord, hear our prayer:
And let our cry come unto you.

Let us pray for the members of the Church in our country, that they may be faithful to the high and holy calling to which God has called his people.

Lord, hear our prayer:
And let our cry come unto you.

Let us pray for ourselves, that in fellowship and service we may show forth the spirit of our Master.

Lord, hear our prayer:
And let our cry come unto you.

Let us pray for the various denominations of the Church, that love may bind them together in unity of purpose in the work of Christ's kingdom.

Lord, hear our prayer:
And let our cry come unto you.

Let us pray for all ministers of the gospel of Christ, that they may be given power to speak the word of the Lord without fear.

Lord, hear our prayer:
And let our cry come unto you. Amen.

41 LET us pray that Christ's Church throughout the world, and especially in this land, may bear fruitful witness through its life and worship.

Lord, hear our prayer:
And let our cry come unto you.

Let us pray for the Church in those countries where there are particular troubles and difficulties at this time; and especially for . . .

Lord, hear our prayer:
And let our cry come unto you.

Let us pray for all who have responsibility in leading the Church, especially for the leaders of denominations represented among us.

Lord, hear our prayer:
And let our cry come unto you.

Let us pray that we may faithfully take our part in the life and work of the Church, now while we are at school, and after we leave.

Lord, hear our prayer:
And let our cry come unto you. Amen.

42 ALMIGHTY and everlasting God, who revealed your glory in Christ, and caused your most holy Word and Gospel to be preached among the people of this land: we pray you to uphold your Church in. . . . Break down all walls that divide your people, and take from them all that may offend your love. Give to the Church new vision and new love; new wisdom and fresh understanding; that the eternal message of your Son may be hailed among us as the good news of this age.
Grant this, O Lord God, through him who makes all things new, Jesus Christ our Lord. *Amen.*

43 O GOD, we pray that your Church, in the midst of troubles and temptations, may remain faithful to your mission.
May your followers, in the midst of persecution and unpopularity, be ready to acknowledge your lordship, and to witness to your gospel of salvation. O God, give them courage, hope, and strength, that they may be able to stand severe tests and overcome all temptations. May they be conscious of the fact that Christ is far above all earthly powers, and can never be overcome.
Help all your servants, and strengthen them, O God. We pray in the name of Jesus, our Lord and Saviour. *Amen.*

BENEDICTIONS

44 UNTO God's gracious mercy and protection we commit ourselves. The Lord bless us and keep us. The Lord make His face to shine upon us and be gracious unto us. The Lord lift up the light of His countenance upon us, and give us peace, both now and for evermore. *Amen.*

45 MAY the blessing of God Almighty, the Father, the Son, and the Holy Spirit rest upon us, and upon all our work and worship done in His Name. May He give us light to guide us, courage to support us, and love to unite us, now and for evermore. *Amen.*

46 MAY God bless us all with a loving sense of His near presence, to guide us, to protect us, and to help us; and may we know what it is to walk close with Him all our life long. *Amen.*

47 MAY the grace of our Lord Jesus Christ, the love of God, and the fellowship of the Holy Spirit be with us all. *Amen.*

OUR LORD'S PRAYER

48 OUR Father who art in heaven,
Hallowed be thy name.
Thy kingdom come,
Thy will be done,
On earth as it is in heaven.
Give us this day our daily bread,
And forgive us our trespasses,
As we forgive those who trespass against us.
And lead us not into temptation.
But deliver us from evil.
For thine is the kingdom, and the power, and the glory
For ever and ever. *Amen.*

New English Form:
OUR Father in heaven,
Your name be hallowed,
Your kingdom come,
Your will be done
On earth as in heaven.
Give us to-day our daily bread.
Forgive us the wrong we have done,
As we have forgiven those who have wronged us.
And do not bring us to the test,
but save us from evil,
for yours is the kingdom,
and the power, and the glory,
for ever. *Amen.*

INDEX OF HYMNS

INDEX OF HYMNS

INDEX OF HYMNS

Note. Hymns with * are also to be found set in tonic sol fa, pp. 228–271

INDEX OF TUNES

Hymn No.	Metre	Tune
33	86.86.86	S.S.B.449, Covenanters
34	77.77.77 (Trochaic)	S.S.B.127, Ministres de l'Eternal
35	77.88 with refrain	B.H.B.134, Resonet in laudibus
36	D.C.M.	B.H.B.115, Bilsdale

HIS DEATH

37	76.76.D	A. & M. (1950) 98, St. Theodulph
38		MS. Spiritual
39	C.M.	B.H.B.205, Mendip
40	L.M.	B.H.B.510, Breslau

HIS RESURRECTION AND VICTORY

41	87.87	E.H.40, Stuttgart
42	77.77 with Aleluyas	B.H.B.157, Easter hymn
43	L.M.	M.H.B.109, Wareham
44	D.S.M.	A. & M. (1950), 149, Old 25th

HIS GLORY, NAME AND PRAISE

*45		Ts. from N., No. 10
*46		A.A.C.M.A.; Tomokudza
47	C.M.	M.H.B.1, Richmond
48	77.77.77	B.H.B.3, Te laudant omnia; or 309, Cassel
49	L.M.	S.P.545, Truro
50	Irregular	S.P.502, Theodoric
51	C.M.	B.H.B.205, Mendip
52	C M	B.H.B.203, St. Peter

THE HOLY SPIRIT
OUR HELPER

*53		Ts. from N., No. 31
54		MS. Yoruba tune
55	77.75	S.S.B.199, Capetown
56	77.77.77	B.H.B.309, Cassel
57	77.77	B.H.B.234, Lübeck
58	65.65	B.H.B.698, Eudoxia
59	C.M.	B.H.B.244, St. Stephen

THE TRINITY

*60		MS. Nsenga tune
*61		MS. Seba Wise, by John Mgandu
62	11.12.12.10	B.H.B.42, Nicaea
63	76.76.D	A. & M. (1950) 625, Erfreut euch; or E.H.594, Gosterwood

Hymn No.	Metre	Tune

BEGINNING AND END OF TERM

119	87.87.87	B.H.B.762, Dismissal
120	87.87.87	B.H.B.372 (2nd tune), Rhuddlan
121	98.89	B.H.B.761 (2nd tune), Randolph

CARE FOR THE ILL OR NEEDY

| 122 | C.M. | B.H.B.634, Ferry |

NATIONAL AND INTERNATIONAL

*123		A.A.C.M.A.; God Bless Africa
124	D.C.M.	E.H.574, Kingsfold
125	C.M.	B.H.B.244, St. Stephen

HELPS TO WORSHIP

*126		A.A.C.M.A.; Missa Mikaeli Mtaka-tifu
*127		MS. Missa Malawi, by V. M. Chunga
*128		MS. (adapted) by Miles Manyonwu, Rhodesia
*129		Risk Collection, No. 44 (Zulu Church)

Hymns with * are also to be found set in tonic sol fa, pp. 228–271

Key

Ts. from N. = Tunes from Nyasaland
E.A.C.C. = East Asia Christian Conference Hymnal
A.A.C.M.A. = All-Africa Church Music Association
MS = Manuscript
M.H.B. = Methodist Hymn Book
S.P. = Songs of Praise
B.H.B. = Baptist Hymn Book
S.S.B. = The School Hymn Book of the Methodist Church
E.H. = English Hymnal
A .& M. (1950) = Hymns Ancient and Modern Revised Edition (1950)
Risk = World Council of Churches Youth Department publication, 1966.